Proceedings

iRODS User Group Meeting 2010

Policy-Based Data Management, Sharing and Preservation

Edited by
Reagan W. Moore
Arcot Rajasekar
Richard Marciano

March 24–26, 2010
University of North Carolina at Chapel Hill, NC, USA

Data Intensive Cyber Environments Center
School of Information and Library Science at UNC Chapel Hill
Renaissance Computing Institute

Data Intensive Cyberinfrastructure Foundation
San Diego

Proceedings of iRODS User Group Meeting 2010

Policy-Based Data Management, Sharing and Preservation

This volume contains contributions to iRODS User Group Meeting 2010, held March 24–26, 2010 at the University of North Carolina at Chapel Hill.

ISBN-13 978-1-452813-42-4

ISBN-10 978-1-452-813-42-4

LCCN 2010906581

Any opinions, findings, conclusions or recommendations expressed in this Proceedings are those of the authors and do not necessarily reflect the views of the authors' institutions or the NSF.

Development of the core iRODS open source software is supported by NSF awards SDCI 0910431 and NARA 0848296.

Acknowledgements: We wish to express our appreciation to the NSF Office of Cyberinfrastructure (OCI) and the National Archives and Records Administration Center for Advanced Systems and Technologies for support and encouragement.

We would also like to acknowledge support from Data Intensive Cyber Environments Center at the University of North Carolina at Chapel Hill; the Renaissance Computing Institute; the School of Information and Library Science at UNC Chapel Hill; and the Data Intensive Cyberinfrastructure Foundation. Proceedings volume edited by Paul Tooby.

Data Intensive Cyberinfrastructure Foundation
For a PDF of this Proceedings see diceresearch.org.

About the cover
Global Data Sharing and Preservation: iRODS, the Integrated Rule-Oriented Data System, is a key component in large-scale projects using "federation" which lets data flow freely between repositories across the nation and around the world. This opens the door to new cross-disciplinary science to solve pressing problems in climate change, biology, astronomy, social science, humanities, and more, as well as long-term archiving and preservation of irreplaceable data. Photograph from Space Shuttle shows clouds and sunlight over the Indian Ocean. Credit: NASA.

Table of Contents

Overview of iRODS User Group Meeting 2010 5
Summary of Papers and Posters 7

1. iRODS User Applications 9
High Availability iRODS System (HAIRS) 11
    Y. Kawai, A. Hasan
iRODS at CC-IN2P3 16
    J-Y Nief, P. Calvat, Y. Cardenas, P-Y Jallud, T. Kachelhoffer
Using iRODS to Preserve and Publish a Dataverse Archive 21
    M. Chua, A. de Torcy, J.H. Ward, J. Crabtree
Conceptualizing Policy-Driven Repository Interoperability Using iRODS and Fedora 25
    D. Pcolar, D.W. Davis, B. Zhu, A. Chassanoff, C-Y Hou, R. Marciano
Community-Driven Development of Preservation Services 32
    R. Marciano, C-Y Hou, J. Ricker, G. McAninch, D. Pcolar, et al

iRODS User Applications – Posters 39
Distributed Data Sharing with PetaShare for Collaborative Research.......................39
    PetaShare Team, LSU
UNC Information Technology Services 41
    W. Schultz
The ARCS Data Fabric 42
    S. Zhang, F. Goessmann, P. Mak
Building a Trusted Distributed Archival Preservation Service with iRODS 44
    J.H. Ward, T.G. Russell, and A. Chassanoff

2. Clients for iRODS 45
A Service-Oriented Interface to the iRODS Data Grid 47
    N. Venuti, F. Locunto, M. Conway, L. Brieger
iExplore for iRODS Distributed Data Management 51
    B. Zhu
The Development of Digital Archives Management Tools for iRODS 53
    T-T Yeh, H-W Wei, S-H Liu, P-C Huang, T-s Hsu, Y-C Chen
A GridFTP Interface for iRODS (poster) 59
    S. Zhang

3. iRODS Integration 61
Enhancing iRODS Integration: Jargon and an Evolving iRODS Service Model 62
    M. Conway

Appendices 67
Appendix 1: Agenda of the iRODS User Group Meeting 2010 69
Appendix 2: iRODS Requested Features 71
Appendix 3: iRODS Clients 75

Overview of iRODS User Group Meeting 2010

iRODS

iRODS, the Integrated Rule-Oriented Data System, is an open source data grid software system developed by the Data Intensive Cyber Environments research group (developers of the SRB, Storage Resource Broker), and collaborators.

The iRODS system, currently at version 2.3, is based on expertise gained through nearly a decade of user-driven applications in support of data grids, digital libraries, persistent archives, and real-time data systems.

iRODS management policies (sets of assertions these communities make about their digital collections) are characterized in iRODS as computer actionable Rules that control the execution of procedures. The procedures are composed from basic functions (micro-services). The state information generated by application of the procedures is stored in a central metadata catalog.

At the iRODS core, a Rule Engine interprets the Rules to decide how the system is to respond to actions initiated by all clients, as well as administrative operations. iRODS is distributed as open source software under a BSD license.

2010 iRODS User Group Meeting

The second annual iRODS user group meeting was held from March 24-26, 2010 in Chapel Hill, North Carolina. The first meeting was held in Nice, France in February 2009. The meeting attracted a wide range of attendees from experienced software developers who are contributing code to the open source iRODS software, to users with installations of varying sizes, to potential users wanting to learn more about iRODS. Users from academia, international and business organizations, and federal and state agencies were represented at the meeting.

With its advanced design and highly configurable and extensible architecture, iRODS is gaining increasing attention and users. The meeting attendance exceeded capacity with attendees from across the United States and as far away as France, Australia, and Taiwan, and participation from Japan by teleconference.

The call for participation encouraged submissions on a wide range of topics, including user applications of iRODS, interoperatibility and clients for accessing the iRODS data system, and integration with other data and repository systems. Contributions include papers, posters, and slides (available on the meeting website at https://www.irods.org/index.php/iRODS_User_Meetings).

The meeting began with sessions on an introduction to release 2.3 of iRODS, descriptions of how to create new micro-services and policies, a review of the unix shell command capabilities (icommands), and descriptions of the interactions (queries) on the iCAT metadata catalog.

A majority of the meeting was devoted to sessions for papers and presentations on user applications. The papers demonstrated the wide range of ways that communities have applied the iRODS framework. More than a dozen presentations and posters described use of iRODS in national data grids (e.g. Australian Research Collaboration Service), large-scale scientific research projects (e.g. KEK high energy physics data grid, French national computing center CC-IN2P3), institutional repositories (e.g. Carolina Digital Repository), and preservation environments (e.g. Taiwan National Archives).

Additional sessions were devoted to the development of new iRODS clients and integration of new capabilities into the iRODS framework. In particular, the JARGON Java I/O library was presented along with plans for integration with web services, development of a dropbox interface (iDrop), and support for digital library interfaces such as Islandora.

The final day of the meeting was dedicated to seeking community input into prioritizing new feature development, and identifying new types of interoperability mechanisms that are needed. A list was compiled of the current clients used to interact with an iRODS data grid. More than 35 existing clients were identified, ranging from Grid clients (GridFTP, JSAGA), file system interfaces (FUSE, PetaFS, webDAV), GUI interfaces (iExplore), digital library interfaces (Fedora, DSpace, Drupal, Islandora), workflow systems (Kepler, Taverna) and specialized interfaces such as URSpace for synchronizing local resources with iRODS. Interactions between collaborators are being supported through the Data Intensive Cyberinfrastructure Foundation, which supports the iRODS open source community.

Benefits to the iRODS Community and Wider Cyberinfrastructure Community

- Interchange among users accelerated the leveraging of each other's applications of iRODS.
- Interchange among users and iRODS developers provided direct user guidance for development of useful real-world features.
- Publication of use cases and other meeting products in the Proceedings for the wider community will disseminate the collective iRODS community expertise.
- Strengthening collaborations with other projects widens interoperability, leveraging the iRODS development investment (see list of 36 current iRODS clients in Appendix).

Summary of Papers and Posters

User Applications: How Communities Have Applied iRODS

Papers

- ***High Availability iRODS System (HAIRS)*** Yutaka Kawai (KEK, Japan), Adil Hasan (University of Liverpool). Describes a High Availability load-balanced iRODS System (HAIRS) developed for use in the KEK high energy physics data grid, with potential applications in similar large-scale scientific research projects.

- ***iRODS at CC-IN2P3*** Jean-Yves Nief, Pascal Calvat, Yonny Cardenas, Pierre-Yves Jallud, Thomas Kachelhoffer (CC-IN2P3, Lyon, France). Describes large scale production use of SRB (2 PB) and iRODS (100s TB) in multiple communities and applications, including data grids in biology and biomedicine; physics; Adonis large-scale humanities community (with Fedora integration); etc. as well as iRODS code development at the French national CC-IN2P3 supercomputing center.

- ***Using iRODS to Preserve and Publish a Dataverse Archive***, Mason Chua (Odum Institute, UNC), Antoine de Torcy (DICE Center, UNC), Jewel H. Ward (SILS, UNC), Jonathan Crabtree (Odum Institute, UNC). Describes interoperation with social science Dataverse Archive, allowing publication of the archive into iRODS to enable search through the iRODS Metadata Catalog (iCAT) and the ability to apply iRODS preservation capabilities to the archive.

- ***Conceptualizing Policy-Driven Repository Interoperability (PoDRI) Using iRODS and Fedora***, David Pcolar (CDR, UNC), Daniel W. Davis (Cornell, DuraSpace), Bing Zhu (DICE, UCSD), Alexandra Chassanoff (SILS, UNC), Chien-Yi Hou, Richard Marciano (SALT, UNC). Describes work to integrate and interoperate between the iRODS and Fedora digital repositories, providing policy-aware object models, including policy expressions, and a distributed architecture for policy-driven management. Combining iRODS and its Rules engine with Fedora's rich semantic object model for digital objects leverages the best features of both products. Funded by IMLS.

- ***Community-Driven Development of Preservation Services***, Richard Marciano (SALT, UNC), Chien-Yi Hou (SALT, UNC), Jennifer Ricker (NC State Library), Glen McAninch (KY Dept. Lib. & Archives), David Pcolar (CDR, UNC) et al. Describes lessons learned in the DCAPE project to articulate a community-based development approach for preservation services that will support institution-specific preservation policies (including business models) while providing required economy of scale for a cost-effective service. Funded by NHPRC.

Posters

- ***Distributed Data Sharing with PetaShare for Collaborative Research***, PetaShare Team @LSU (poster). Describes use of iRODS in the PetaShare data grid to enable transparent handling of data sharing, archival, and retrieval mechanisms, making data easily available to scientists for analysis and visualization on demand. Used in 25 research projects in five state universities and two health sciences centers across Louisiana. Describes the PetaFs virtual filesystem.

- ***University of North Carolina Information Technology Services***, William Schultz (UNC) (poster). Describes use of iRODS in multiple data grids in the context of UNC HPC infrastructure.

- ***The ARCS Data Fabric***, Shunde Zhang, Florian Goessmann, Pauline Mak (ARCS) (poster). Describes use of iRODS in the ARCS Data Fabric which lets researchers easily store and share research data across institutional boundaries in a generic service not tied to any specific kinds of data or research disciplines and available to every Australian researcher and international collaborators. Describes access through WebDAV clients.

- ***Building a Trusted Distributed Archival Preservation Service with iRODS***, Jewel H. Ward, Terrell G. Russell, and Alexandra Chassanoff (SILS, UNC) (poster). Describes design and development of generic iRODS Rules to 1) validate the trustworthiness of a repository through the enactment of ISO-MOIMS compliant policies; and 2) enable the distributed auditable administration of the repository through the invocation of iRODS Rules.

Clients for iRODS

Papers

- ***A Service-Oriented Interface to the iRODS Data Grid***, Nicola Venuti, Francesco Locunto (NICE), Michael Conway, Leesa Brieger (UNC RENCI and DICE). Describes an open source iRODS plugin that gives iRODS users access to the Nice EnginFrame cloud interface framework through an easy-to-use GUI that can be easily customized for community use, offering multiple views for users, administrators, etc.

- ***iExplore for iRODS Distributed Data Management***, Bing Zhu (DICE group, UCSD). Describes the iExplore GUI client tool for navigation and manipulation of data within the iRODS distributed data system. Designed and implemented in the Windows platform, it offers a rich set of functions and excellent performance.

- ***The Development of Digital Archives Management Tools for iRODS,*** Tsung-Tai Yeh, Hsin-Wen Wei, Shin-Hao Liu (Academia Sinica, Taiwan), Pei-Chi Huang (Tsing Hua University, Taiwan), Tsan-sheng Hsu (Academia Sinica, Taiwan), Yen-Chiu Chen (Tsing Hua University, Taiwan). Describes development for use in the TELDAP program in Taiwan of the UrSpace user interface and corresponding Sync Package and monitoring system (SIMS) that can check iRODS for errors and monitor the system independently.

Posters

- ***A GridFTP Interface for iRODS***, Shunde Zhang (ARCS). Describes the design and implementation of a GridFTP interface for iRODS. Written as a plugin on Globus GridFTP for iRODS, it provides an OS-independent standalone solution that doesn't rely on Globus but is compatible with existing Globus clients.

iRODS Integration

- ***Enhancing iRODS Integration: Jargon and an Evolving iRODS Service Model,*** Mike Conway (DICE Center, UNC). Describes the JARGON Java I/O library and plans for integration with web services, development of a dropbox interface (iDrop), and support for digital library interfaces such as Islandora.

1. iRODS User Applications

High Availability iRODS System (HAIRS)

Yutaka Kawai, *Adil Hasan***

*Computing Research Center, High Energy Accelerator Research Organization (KEK)
**School of English, University of Liverpool

Abstract

The integrated Rule Oriented Data Management System (iRODS) is a policy-driven data management system that is starting to be used by projects with large data volume requirements that require a highly available system. In this paper we describe an approach to provide a Highly Availability load-balanced iRODS System (HAIRS). We also describe the advantages and disadvantages of the approach and future work.

Index Keyword Terms—High Availability, Ultra–Monkey, PgPool, Director, ldirectord, ipvsadm

1. Introduction

The integrated Rule Oriented Data Management System (iRODS) [6] is an open-source, policy-driven distributed data management system developed by the Data Intensive Cyber Environments group that insulates its' users from changes to the physical components of the system. Interaction with data stored in the iRODS system is done using logical file-names and storage names. The iRODS system takes care of the translation from the logical to the physical name. Changes to the physical location of a file only requires the logical-to-physical file mapping to be updated.

Changes to the physical storage resource require an update to the logical-to-physical storage resource mapping and, if required, the implementation of a new iRODS driver that is able to translate iRODS file commands to those used by the physical storage resource. In this way iRODS provides a uniform interface to heterogeneous storage resources. In addition to a virtual file-system iRODS also provides the possibility to impose a series of directives (collective called policies, or rules) on the data stored. In keeping with the iRODS philosophy the rules are defined in a high-level, fully-featured language with each step of the rule implemented as a C-base service (termed a micro-service).The rule is insulated from changes to the underlying micro-services.

An iRODS system consists of one iRODS server that communicates directly with the iRODS Metadata Catalog (iCAT) database and an iRODS server running on each storage resource. All iRODS servers require an iRODS rule engine that executes the triggered rules. An iRODS system can be federated with another iRODS system providing seamless access to data stored in a remote iRODS system. The iRODS is starting to be used by projects with large numbers of users and with large data volume requirements in Japan [10, 11, 14], France [10, 4], the USA [10, 18] and Australia [1]. Such projects operate in an 'always-on' mode and cannot tolerate a failure in accessing the data. Within iRODS a failure of a single storage resource can be mitigated by replicating the data over more than one resource. But, the iCAT and the iCAT-enabled iRODS server remain as a single point of failure. If the iCAT database is down, or if the iCAT enabled server is offline the iRODS system cannot be used.

In Section 2 we describe the approach of database replication to mitigate against iCAT server failure and in Sections 3 we describe the approaches to mitigate against iCAT-enabled server failure. Section 4 describes some of the tests we performed in order to determine the impact of the approach and Section 5 outlines future work.

2. Redundant iCAT

The iRODS Metadata Catalogue (iCAT) contains all the information necessary to manage files stored in iRODS. The iCAT is implemented as a set of tables in a PostgreSQL, ORACLE or MySQL database. Only one iCAT exists per iRODS system and, as such, forms a single point of failure. Implementing database replication techniques can eliminate this critical point.

The Australian Research Collaborative Service has implemented PostgreSQL database replication for the iCAT using PgPool [9]. The procedure essentially requires setting up two iCAT PostgreSQL databases that are replicated via PgPool as shown in figure 1. The iCAT databases are interfaced to two iRODS servers A and B, and clients can connect to either server. Any changes to either iCAT are

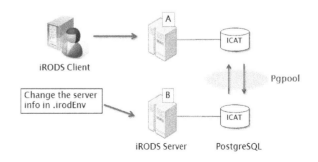

Figure 1. iRODS High Availability using PgPool.

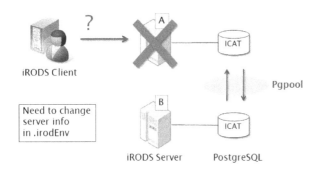

Figure 2. Failure situation: iRODS server A is down.

automatically replicated to the other iCAT.

A similar approach can be used for an iRODS that uses MySQL [16], while Oracle provides its own mechanisms for replicating databases [15].

This approach is extremely useful for creating a fault-tolerant iCAT although it requires the client to actively know which iRODS-enabled ICAT server they are connected to and to alter their configuration if their default server is down (see figure 2). In Section 3 we describe an approach that addresses this problem.

3. Redundant iCAT Enabled iRODS Server

An iRODS consists of only one iRODS server that interfaces to the iCAT. Like the iCAT this server is also a critical component of the iRODS and redundancy of this server would eliminate this single point of failure. By making use of a load-balancer application [12] one can create a redundant pool of servers with a single point of entry for the client application. In this way the client does not need to remember which set of servers belong to the pool and new servers can be added to the pool as required allowing the system to scale with increasing load.

There are a number of load-balancers available that enable a redundant system to be built, these split along hardware or software lines. For example, the CISCO CATALYST 6500 [2] hardware component, can do Layer 4 switching and has load-balancing algorithms. Hardware load-balancers are high-performance, robust and tend to be expensive. Examples of software load-balancers are HAProxy [3] that supports http, ssh etc protocols and Ultra Monkey [17] that provides support for a wide range of protocols. At the time of writing HAProxy does not provide support for simple-TCP based protocols on which the iRODS protocol is based and so Ultra Monkey was used in this study.

The approach used in this paper is to make use of a software load-balancer and adapt it to provide a pool of iCAT enabled iRODS servers that are mapped to a virtual server which the client connects to. This approach ensures that if one server is unavailable the client will be directed to the next available server.

Ultra Monkey is a Linux-based load-balancer that makes use of Linux Virtual Server [13] to provide a fast load-balancer implemented as the Linux Director as shown in figure 3. The Linux Director ideally runs on a separate server and essentially contains a list of real servers which are regularly polled. Clients connect to the director which then forwards requests to the least loaded server. If one of the servers is overloaded or down the client is automatically redirected to another server in the pool. The Linux Director is only used to establish a connection between the client and the least-loaded, working iRODS server. Once the connection has been established iRODS takes over to complete the interaction. This ensures that the extra cost (in time) due to the Linux Director is minimal.

In this way the iRODS system can scale with increasing load as new iRODS servers can be added to the pool as needed without the client needing to update their configuration. The following sections describe the load-balancer setup used in this work.

3.1. Network Configuration

The network configuration of the load-balancer is shown in figure 4 and in tables 1 and 2. The Linux Director is installed on a separate server and behaves as a virtual iRODS server that maps the client request to a real iRODS server (it behaves effectively as a Network Address Translation device). The Linux Director and the iRODS servers need to be in the same domain as the load-balancer cannot span different domains (i.e. the Linux Director cannot load-balance over a pool of servers that are located in different administrative domains).

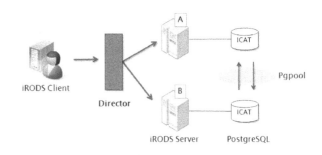

Figure 3. Solution using Director.

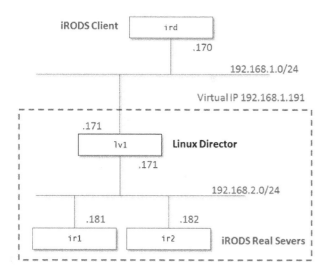

iRODS Client

ird

.170

192.168.1.0/24

Virtual IP 192.168.1.191

.171

lv1   **Linux Director**

.171

192.168.2.0/24

.181   .182

ir1   ir2   **iRODS Real Severs**

Figure 4. Example: Network Configuration

IP address	Description
192.168.1.171	Linux Director for 192.168.1.0/24 network
192.168.1.191	Virtual Server
192.168.1.170	iRODS Client

Table 1. Network 192.168.1.0/24

IP address	Description
192.168.1.171	Linux Director for 192.168.2.0/24 network
192.168.1.191	iRODS Real Server 1
192.168.1.170	iRODS Real Server 2

Table 2. Network 192.168.2.0/24

3.2. Linux Director Installation

The Linux Director was installed on a CentOS5 Linux server. In addition to the Linux Director server application the following applications need to be installed (more details can be found on the Ultra Monkey web site [17]):

- heartbeat: runs on the Linux Director server and polls the iRODS servers to determine their load.
- heartbeat-ldirectord: interfaces the heartbeat application to the Linux Director to allow clients to be directed to the least loaded server.
- heartbeat-pils: plug-in interface application to interface to the Linux Director.
- heartbeat-stonith: used to remotely power down a node in the pool.
- Ipvsadm: administers IP virtual server services offered by the Linux kernel.

- Libnet: utilities to help with managing network packets.

```
<MsgHeader_PI>
<type>RODS_VERSION</type>
<msgLen>182</msgLen>
<errorLen>0</errorLen>
<bsLen>0</bsLen>
<intInfo>0</intInfo>
</MsgHeader_PI>
<Version_PI>
<status>-4000</status>
<relVersion>rods2.1</relVersion>
<apiVersion>d</apiVersion>
<reconnPort>0</reconnPort>
<reconnAddr></reconnAddr>
<cookie>0</cookie>
</Version_PI>
```

Figure 5. Routine strings iRODS server returns

There are several things to care about when installing the Linux Director for an iRODS system. The Linux Director daemon ldirectord reads its configurations from the configuration file ldirectord.cf which, by default is be installed in /etc/ha.d. The configuration file contains the list of iRODS servers that the Linux Director must map the client to. In order for Ultra Monkey to work with the iRODS protocol the "service" flag in the ldirectord.cf file should be "simpletcp". The iRODS server returns routine messages whenever it receives any message from a client (figure 5). Therefore, the "request" flag in the ldirectord.cf can contain any client request (the iRODS ils client command was used as this interacted with the metadata catalogue and ensured the whole system was functioning). The "receive" flag should be specified as "RODS VERSION" which is a part of the iRODS server response. An example of the ldirectord.cf file is shown in figure 6.

```
checktimeout=10
checkinterval=2
autoreload=yes
logfile="/var/log/ldirectord.log"
logfile="local0"
quiescent=no

virtual=192.168.1.191:1247
        real=192.168.2.181:1247 masq
        real=192.168.2.182:1247 masq
        protocol=tcp
        service=simpletcp
        request="test"
        receive="RODS_VERSION"
        scheduler=lc
        checktype=negotiate
        netmask=255.255.255.255
```

Figure 6. An example of ldirectord.cf.

The ipvsadm (Linux Virtual Server administration) command can have one of ten types of scheduling-method [5]. It is configured by the flag "scheduler", table 3 shows a list of the scheduling methods ldirectord can configure. The ldirectord configuration in the figure 6 specifies "lc" to assign more jobs to real servers with fewer active jobs.

Scheduler Flag	Scheduling Method
rr	Round Robin
wrr	Weighted Round Robin
lc	Least-Connection
wls	Weighted Least-Connection
lblc	Locality-Based Least-Connection
lblcr	Locality-Based Least-Connection with Replication
dh	Destination Hashing
sh	Source Hashing
sed	Shortest Expected Delay
nq	Never Queue

Table 3. ipvsadm scheduling-method Algorithm.

4. Tests

In this section we describe the tests carried out to determine the performance impact of the load-balancer. The first test addresses the impact of the load-balancer on the transfer of large files and the second concerns the overhead the load-balancer places on client interaction with the iRODS server. Both tests made use of the client C-based iRODS utilities ("icommands") that form part of the iRODS suite [8].

4.1. Large File Transfer

The "iput" command is used to store a file into an iRODS system. By default, if the file size is larger than 32 MB, iput performs the transfer in parallel [7]. In this case the data transfer is carried out directly between the physical resource and the client as shown in figure 7:

1. Client issues iput with a large file.
2. Server A finds the physical location to store the file.
3. Server A directs the other iRODS Server C with the physical storage to open parallel I/O ports.
4. File transfer starts between Client and Server C.

Redundancy of iRODS storage servers is provided by replicating data over more than one storage server and so the load-balancer does not need to be configured to provide redundancy for these servers; only for the iRODS iCAT-enabled server. This greatly simplifies the configuration as shown in figure 8 as the ports that the large file transfers occur on do not need to be mapped in the Linux Director configuration.

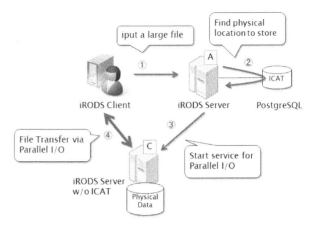

Figure 7. Large file transfer: Normal case.

The configuration is almost exactly as in figure 7 except that the Linux Director forwards the client connection to an iRODS server which then forwards the request to the target storage system. This setup limits the complexity of the configuration of the Linux Director and eliminates the impact of the load-balancer on the transfer of large files. In our tests files of 1GB in size were successfully stored in iRODS with the client.

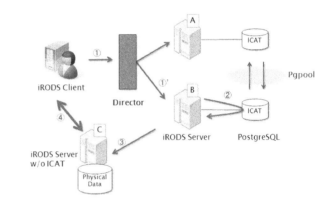

Figure 8. Large file transfer: The case using director.

4.2. Load-balancer Overhead

The iRODS suite contains a package for performing concurrent tests on an iRODS system. This package was used to understand the overhead the load-balancer places on an iRODS system. The concurrent test sequentially executes several icommands, iput (to store data), imeta (to query the metadata catalogue), iget (to retrieve data), and imv (to move data from one iRODS resource to another). The concurrent tests were performed for 1, 10, 50 and 100-1000 clients. The network configuration is the same as the example in the previous sections (figure 4). Physically, all the iRODS servers are Xen virtual machines on the same physical machine and the only iRODS client is on the different physical machine. This can have a non-trivial and noticeable effect on the results of the tests.

Three series of tests were performed to understand the impact of the load-balancer:

case1: Normal case. The iRODS client directly accesses one iRODS server.
case2: Using a director. The iRODS client accesses one iRODS server through the Linux Director.
case3: Load sharing case. The iRODS client accesses two iRODS servers through the Linux Director.

In order to get the average values, the concurrent-test program is executed three times for each test. The figure 9 shows the results of the tests. The case 2 is about 10% slower than the normal case 1 so the impact of the speed performance by using director should be considered. However, while considering optimization of Director implementation, controlling tradeoff between access speed and benefits of high availability becomes practical.

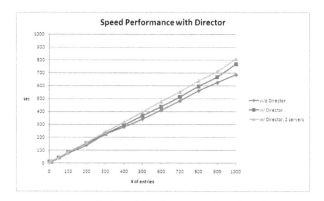

Figure 9. Speed Performance Test Results.

5. Conclusion and Future work

This paper has described how a highly available iRODS system can be implemented with a load-balancer with negligible impact to the client. The impact of the load-balancer on the performance of the iRODS system is minimal and should be considered in the case where a highly available system is needed. Although the approach described was for the Ultra Monkey load-balancer we believe the same approach can be used for any other load-balancer. In addition this approach can also result in a highly scalable iRODS system that can grow with increasing load.

One area that we consider to be limiting is the restriction of the redundant iRODS servers to be within the same domain. A truly high availability system would try to eliminate domain-specific problems by having a pool of servers that span multiple domains. This is an area we are looking at addressing in the future. We are also looking at applying the concept of HAIRS to other catalog services such as the RNS (Resource Namespace Service) application, Gfarm (Grid Data Farm), etc.

6. Acknowledgment

The authors would like to thank to Prof.Takashi Sasaki and Yoshimi Iida. Prof.Sasaki coordinated the study. Ms.Iida gave us valuable support for the iRODS setup in KEK. Adil Hasan is also grateful to the KEK institute for their kind hospitality and to the KEK Short-term Visiting Scientist program financial support during the course of this study.

7. References

[1] Australian Research Collaboration Service. Online. http://projects.arcs.org.au/trac/podd/wiki/iRODS.
[2] CISCO CATALYST 6500 SERIES CONTENT SWITCHING MODULE. Online. http://www.cisco.com/en/US/products/hw/modules/ps2706/produ cts_data_sheet09186a00800887f3.html.
[3] HAProxy - The Reliable, High Performance TCP/HTTP Load Balancer. Online. http://haproxy.1wt.eu/.
[4] IN2P3 – National Institute of Nuclear Physics and Particle Physics. Online. http://cc.in2p3.fr/?lang=en.
[5] ipvsadm(8) - Linux man page, scheduler option. Online. http://linux.die.net/man/8/ipvsadm.
[6] iRODS – the Integrated Rule-Oriented Data System. Online. http://www.irods.org.
[7] iRODS file transfer. Online. https://www.irods.org/index.php/iRods_file_transfer.
[8] iRODS icommands. Online. https://www.irods.org/index.php/icommands.
[9] iRODS Master/Slave Replication with pgpool. Online. https://projects.arcs.org.au/trac/systems/wiki/DataServices/iRODS _Replication_Pgpool.
[10] Projects Using and Developing iRODS. Online. http://www.diceresearch.org/DICE_Site/iRODS_Uses.html.
[11] KEK – High Energy Accelerator Research Organization, KEK. Online. http://www.kek.jp/intra-e/index.html.
[12] Load balancing (computing). http://en.wikipedia.org/wiki/Load_balancing_%28computing%29
[13] The Linux Virtual Server. Online. http://www.linuxvirtualserver.org/.
[14] Lyon-KEK. Online. https://www.irods.org/index.php/Lyon-KEK.
[15] P. McElroy and M. Pratt. Oracle Database 11g: Oracle Streams Replication. Technical report, Oracle, 2007. http://www.oracle.com/technology/products/dataint/pdf/twp_strea ms_replication_11gr1.pdf.
[16] MySQL Master Master Replication. Online. http://www.howtoforge.com/mysql_master_master_replication
[17] UltraMonkey, Load Balancing and High Availability Solution. Online. http://www.ultramonkey.org/.
[18] Information Technology Services for The University of North Carolina at Chapel Hill. Online. http://its.unc.edu/its/index.htm.

iRODS at CC-IN2P3

Jean-Yves Nief, Pascal Calvat, Yonny Cardenas, Pierre-Yves Jallud, Thomas Kachelhoffer
CC-IN2P3, CNRS USR 6402, Villeurbanne, France

Abstract

In this paper, we will show how iRODS is being used at CC-IN2P3, the future plans, code development, and also SRB to iRODS migration.

1. Introduction

CC-IN2P3 [1] is a national computing centre located in Lyon (France) which is dedicated to high energy physics, nuclear physics, astrophysics and now is involved in Arts and Humanities projects as well as biology and biomedical applications. It provides computing, storage resources and other services to the French and international scientific community.

iRODS, like its predecessor SRB, is a key service for CC-IN2P3 as it provides the ability to manage large amounts of data which can be distributed across other data centers. These data, produced by instruments or computing simulations, can be accessed and shared from anywhere when scientists within the same experiment or project are spread around the world.

In this paper, we will show how iRODS is used in production and how its usage will evolve in the near future. We will also describe the participation of CC-IN2P3 in the iRODS code development as well as a Java explorer. As SRB is still heavily used in production for several experiments and projects, we will describe plans for the SRB to iRODS migration.

2. iRODS in Production

1.1 Hardware and software setup

The iRODS service at CC-IN2P3 is supported by 10 servers. It includes:

- 2 servers used to host the iCAT servers: Linux boxes running Scientific Linux 4 and 5 operating system.
- 6 servers are used as non-iCAT servers which are hosting the data: These are Sun X4540 servers on Solaris 10 operating system, ZFS is used for the file system storing files in iRODS. There is a total of 200 TB of disk space available.
- 2 Linux boxes are used to host the Oracle 11g database cluster which is hosting the iCAT databases.

Each project or experiment has its own iRODS instance running on a given port number. Therefore the hardware is shared by all the users of the iRODS service.

The iCAT server is vital to the service. It is a single point of failure and therefore redundancy is needed. To mitigate this we have duplicated the iRODS iCAT servers on two machines which are seen under a unique name DNS alias called "ccirods": this DNS load-balanced alias is based on software developed at SLAC. Client applications connect to the service through this DNS load-balanced alias.

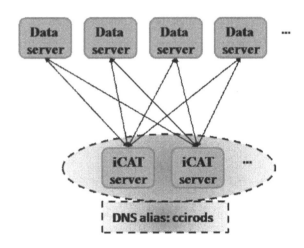

Figure 1: Hardware setup.

We are planning to host more data than can be accommodated by the data servers, and part of the files registered in iRODS will end up on tapes. Therefore the iRODS data servers will be interfaced with HPSS, our Mass Storage System, using the universal Mass Storage driver developed at CC-IN2P3. The transfer protocol used for data migration between iRODS and HPSS is RFIO.

For some projects, parts of their data are unique and must not be lost under any circumstances. We have decided to use Tivoli Storage Manager to do the backup of these files. Other copies of these files are double copied on tapes located in our computing facility as well as another building on campus. We could have used iRODS data replication functionalities with servers located in the other building, but this solution would have been more expensive and was not required, as data can be restored quickly with our current system.

Servers' health is checked every 30 minutes using Nagios probes which test whether the iRODS instances are responding properly to iRODS connection attempts. In case of server reboot or daemons disappearance, the servers are restarted automatically by cron tasks.

A report of iRODS usage (number of files, amount of storage space) by users, groups, and experiments is made on a daily basis. The results are reported in our MRTG system and available to all iRODS authenticated users.

1.2 Usage examples

iRODS has been in production since 2008 for a few large projects that we will describe briefly in this section.

1.2.1 TIDRA

TIDRA stands for «Traitement Informatique Distribué en Rhône-Alpes». This is the Rhône-Alpes area data grid which federates computing resources in five laboratories spread across Lyon, Grenoble, and Annecy campus, with CC-IN2P3 as the main data center. TIDRA provides computing resources for the Rhône-Alpes scientific community, and iRODS is a key component for the storage and data management part.

It is used in biology applications (phylogeny): jobs are submitted on the grid and access data from iRODS and store job output back into iRODS at a high rate. The number of connections on the iRODS cluster has reached 60,000 per day, with aggregate network activity up to 2 Gbits/s: no obvious limitations have been noticed and therefore I/O activity can be increased without any anticipated problems.

It is also used in biomedical applications such as animal imagery (mice) and human data (heart and lung studies). For DICOM files, the extraction of the header metadata is being done using DCMTK [2], a DICOM toolkit. The metadata are then registered into iRODS in a bulk mode. All these steps are included in a Rule that is triggered automatically on the iRODS server side every time a DICOM file is registered into the system. This allows researchers to search for a data subset based on some metadata criteria.

Other users are expected to use iRODS in the near future, such as researchers from the synchrotron facility in Grenoble (ESRF [3]). There are already 15 users and 3 million files registered in the catalog and we expect to host 20 TB of data by the end of 2010.

1.2.2 Adonis

Adonis [4] is a French national funded project which aims to federate and provide a platform of computing services for the Arts and Humanities national community. Adonis is also connected to European projects like DARIA.

Various projects within Adonis are already using iRODS, which is one of the key services. There are various needs: archival of documents from the Middle Age: data access from batch processing farms (riverbed studies in geography, movie simulations of ancient monuments). iRODS will be also used for data access through web sites,

easing web site code development and avoiding having to modify legacy web applications which will be hosted at CC-IN2P3. Fuse-iRODS allows mounting iRODS collection trees as a regular file system on the servers, therefore it is well suited in the present case to adapt web applications to data access through iRODS, without having to change a single line of code.

One of the main Adonis project is to provide a platform to make long-term preservation of data produced by research laboratories spread across France into CINES [5], a national computing facility in Montpellier, and then provide online data access through Fedora-Commons [6] at CC-IN2P3. In the example below (Fig. 2), audio files are produced by researchers from CRDO (Paris). The data are pushed to CINES where they are archived. The files that belong to the same object (i.e. the same family) are pushed in tar balls to CC-IN2P3 using iRODS. On the iRODS servers in Lyon, the files in the tar ball are extracted and registered automatically in Fedora-Commons using an iRODS Rule triggered automatically. The Fedora-Commons storage back end is iRODS: this is achieved using a Fuse-iRODS mount point on the Fedora-Commons server. It was the most obvious way of interfacing iRODS with Fedora-Commons as the present Java interface between the two does not have all needed functionalities. In a future version of the workflow, it is foreseen to also have an iRODS server in CINES, so that once the data produced by any research lab is pushed into iRODS, even the second step of the workflow, i.e. data preservation, would be triggered automatically using iRODS Rules.

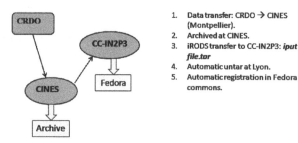

1. Data transfer: CRDO → CINES (Montpellier).
2. Archived at CINES.
3. iRODS transfer to CC-IN2P3: *iput file.tar*
4. Automatic untar at Lyon.
5. Automatic registration in Fedora commons.

Figure 2: Adonis preservation and publication workflow.

There are already 20 TB of data stored in iRODS, representing 2 million files. This will increase to more than 100 TB by the end of 2010.

1.3 Prospects for 2010

iRODS is being adopted by many projects in various fields hosted at CC-IN2P3. They have already started to use iRODS or will start soon. Here is a non-exhaustive list:

- Biology: phylogeny.
- Biomedical applications: animal imagery, cardiology, neuroscience using magnetoencephalography,

positron emission tomography, fMRI, X-ray and gamma ray imagery.

- Astrophysics: LSST [7], JEM-EUSO.
- High Energy Physics: dChooz [8] (neutrino experiment).
- Arts and Humanities: Adonis.

We estimate that iRODS services at CC-IN2P3 will host at least 300 TB of data by the end of 2010. This does not include some projects which are using SRB at the moment and that will migrate to iRODS this year. The petabyte scale will be reached in the near future. Some issues with file names which can potentially contain accented letters must be solved in the area of Arts and Humanities.

3. Code Development

In this section, we describe our participation in iRODS code development (author: Jean-Yves Nief) and also a Java-based GUI interface called JUX which can be used to browse iRODS, among other protocols (author: Pascal Calvat).

2.1 Scripts

A script has been developed to test iCommand functionalities and ensure that they are behaving as expected: it allows checking that no obvious bug shows up before a new iRODS software version is released.

Another script has been written to do stress tests by launching in parallel a certain number of iRODS operations and measuring the time response of the system.

All these scripts need to be updated as the number of iRODS features has increased significantly in the recent past.

2.2 Micro-services and iCommands

A set of Micro-services has been written for several purposes:

- **Access control**: This is a flexible firewall that can be tuned using a configuration file located in *server/config*. It prevents iRODS connections from any set of machines and for any user or group of users that has been specified in the configuration file. It can be triggered simply by using the *acChkHostAccessControl* hook in *core.irb*.
- **Tar file creation and tar file extraction**: these Micro-services can create a tar file from a given output collection and register it automatically into iRODS, and they can extract files from a tar ball registered into iRODS and put the content of the tar archive into a given output collection.
- **Access rights setting**: Sets the access rights on a given input collection or a file.

- **Resource Monitoring system Micro-services**: these will be described in more detail in the subsection below.

An iCommand called iscan has been created: it checks if a local data object or a local directory content is registered in iRODS. This tool is intended for administrators to look for orphan objects on iRODS data servers (i.e. objects not registered in iRODS).

2.3 Universal Mass Storage System driver

The goal of this driver is to interface iRODS with any kind of Mass Storage System or any other storage system, using the communication protocol of the administrator's choice (e.g: pftp, rfio, gridftp, hpss etc.) based on the shell commands they are already using. It is an easy way to quickly interface an existing storage system with iRODS without having to use the storage system APIs. This can save time in code development and more importantly users can continue to access this Mass Storage System using the same tools they have been using for direct access, therefore allowing users to maintain a homogeneous way of accessing their MSS system.

This is very flexible and highly configurable on the system and can be configured to provide, for example, HPSS access in a similar manner as the built-in HPSS driver (which uses client libraries to interface). In both HPSS cases, files will be cached between iRODS and HPSS: using compound resources to handle MSS resources is mandatory when using this driver as no direct access to the MSS for the iRODS client is allowed.

Resource Monitoring System

The resource monitoring system has two goals:

- It provides a monitoring system of the servers' activity for a given federation of iRODS servers: it measures the load of each server at a given frequency. The measured quantities are the CPU load, runq load, memory usage, swap memory usage, paging I/O activity, network activity, and disk occupancy on the file systems used by the iRODS physical resources.
- It provides a load balancing system: it gives a measure of the load of each server based on the information extracted above. This information can subsequently be used to choose one physical resource among others for put/get operations.

For monitoring server activity (Fig. 3), a Rule is being executed at a given frequency (say every 10 minutes) and starts a Micro-service called *msiServerMonPerf*. This Micro-service will trigger execution of the script *irodsServerMonPerf* on all (or a subset of) the iRODS servers having physical resources declared: the action is launched on all the target servers at the same time. The *irodsServerMonPerf* script will measure the quantities described above (e.g. CPU load, memory usage etc.): each quantity is an integer with a value between 0 and 100 (e.g.: CPU load = 0 means that no CPU is used, CPU load = 100 means that 100% of the CPU is used). Once the script has finished, all measurements are stored in a dedicated iCAT table and are used subsequently by other Micro-services described below.

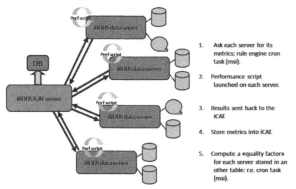

Figure 3: RMS in action.

For the load-balancing system, a Rule is executed at a given frequency (say every 10 minutes) and starts a Micro-service called *msiDigestMonStat* that computes a load factor for each server. This load factor has a value between 0 and 100: a higher number corresponds to a higher server load. This load factor is computed based on the measured quantities above:

$$load = (\alpha \times CPUload + \beta \times MEMload +$$
$$\gamma \times RUNQload + \delta \times SWAPload +$$
$$\varepsilon \times PAGEIOload + \theta \times NETload +$$
$$\mu \times DISKused)/7$$

where α, β, γ, δ, ε, θ and μ must be between 0 and 1 and must be set by the administrator. For instance, if one wants to choose servers based on the CPU load and the network load criteria, then α=0.5 and θ=0.5; all the other factors have to be set to 0. The load factor is stored into a dedicated iCAT table. It can then be used directly by hooks like *acSetRescSchemeForCreate* to pick out the least loaded physical resource within a list of resources.

The remote monitoring system also updates some physical resource metadata such as the disk space available and the resource status, i.e. if it is up and running, or down because it is unreachable.

2.4 JUX

JUX [9] stands for "Java Universal eXplorer". The main purpose of JUX is to provide a single Graphical User Interface written in Java to access data stored on different kind of data grids. JUX is intuitive and easy-to-use for non-expert users. Its uncluttered interface uses contextual menus and features like "drag and drop", and is close to widely used explorers such as the Windows Explorer. There are similar tools to JUX such as Hermes [10] developed by James Cook University (Australia) and VBrowser [11] developed by the Virtual Lab for e-Science (Netherlands) which are based on Apache Commons VFS.

JUX is based on the Java implementation of the SAGA specifications called JSAGA [12] and developed by Sylvain Reynaud at CC-IN2P3. JSAGA provides a data management layer as well as security mechanisms. It allows JUX to connect with many different protocols such as iRODS, SRB, gsiftp, SRM, http, sftp, zip, and local file systems using security mechanisms such as login/password or X509 certificates. An iRODS plugin to JSAGA had to be written using Jargon APIs. Files can be copied from one system such as SRB to another such as iRODS in a single "drag and drop". With JUX, it is also possible to display the content of a file (ascii, pictures, audio files) as well as iRODS metadata attached to it (fig. 4). It will be soon possible to search files based on metadata criteria.

Figure 4: Example of JUX display.

4. SRB to iRODS migration

The SRB to iRODS migration is an important topic for CC-IN2P3 as SRB is still heavily used.

3.1 SRB usage at CC-IN2P3

Since 2003 the Storage Resource Broker has been used by more than 10 projects and experiments, from high energy physics and nuclear physics, to astroparticle physics, biology and biomedical applications. SRB is a key component of these international projects as CC-IN2P3 plays a major role for them, whether as the central repository or mirror site: SRB is the main repository and means of data access and management for them.

SRB handles more than 2 PB of data on both disk and tape, hundreds of thousands of connections per day, a daily network traffic that can reach 15 to 20 TB. SRB clients span from laptops to supercomputers (e.g. IBM BlueGene), on a wide range of Operating Systems (Windows, Mac

OSX, Linux, AIX, Solaris). In order to access the SRB, they use either Scommands (equivalent to iCommands), Java APIs (Jargon), or web services. Connections to SRB come from all over Europe and from as far as Hawaii and Australia. SRB is still growing and will reach 3 PB of data managed by the end of this year.

Among the biggest users are:
- BaBar [13]: a High Energy Physics experiment based at SLAC (Stanford). Data analysis is being performed both at the SLAC computing centre and also at CC-IN2P3. In order to have full data access to end users in Lyon, we designed a two zone system, with automatic synchronization of data between the two sites, allowing receiving newly produced data from the BaBar detector and simulation data at CC-IN2P3 within 24 to 48 hours. Once this system was set up, it has been able to transfer up to 5 TB of data per day from SLAC tapes to CC-IN2P3 tapes, with a minimal amount of manpower and maintenance work. Three million files, corresponding to more than 1 PB of data have been transferred in this way.

- Lattice QCD: this field of theoretical physics produces vast amounts of data. CC-IN2P3 hosts the largest QCD repository in Europe with more than 1 PB stored. These data are produced and accessed from several computing centers in France, Germany, and the Netherlands.

The scalability and reliability of SRB has proven to be extremely important in fulfilling the needs of these experiments. SRB has been a key point for their success.

3.2 Migration Plan to iRODS

SRB is a central tool for these experiments, it is heavily used on a daily basis. Therefore, the migration from SRB to iRODS in this production environment must be handled carefully as we need to have minimal disturbances in the process. For projects using Jargon APIs for their client applications, it will be fairly easy and require a minimum amount of work. But the other projects are using shell, Perl, or Python scripts using the Scommands. This will require more work as these scripts can be spread through various parts of the software tools written for the project, and also in the code of the end users. In order to make this migration less painful we are planning to write a small utility that will parse user scripts and detect lines where Scommands need to be replaced by iCommands.

We will begin this migration process this year with BioEmergences [14] (60 TB of data by the end of 2010). We will continue with other projects in the next two years, and hope to finish the migration by the end of 2012. We will not do the migration for projects that have already finished taking data within the last two years: this is the case of BaBar and Supernovae Factory [15].

5. Conclusion

SRB has proven to be a powerful data management tool that can be easily adapted to many different needs. It is highly scalable and robust. It is an important requirement for scientific data management as the amount of data and metadata increase at a huge rate. We are now at the scale of the Petabyte, and in just a few years will reach the Exabyte level.

iRODS, with its ability to handle complex data workflows goes far beyond the functionalities of the SRB and any other grid middleware tool. The iRODS Rule mechanism offers a wide range of solutions for data management and great flexibility to adapt to any needs: it can interact in a transparent manner with a large amount of third party software and data storage systems. Its unique features are very appealing for many users, and their feedback so far has been extremely positive. We are also confident that iRODS is well-suited for projects handling hundreds of petabytes and hundreds of millions of files. iRODS is very easy to install on any platform and requires very little maintenance as it is a robust tool. This is a major requirement for CC-IN2P3: a manpower-consuming tool could be an important show stopper for our projects.

We expect to quickly reach the Petabyte scale for iRODS within a year, with an increased number of projects using it. Other developments are envisaged, especially for the Resource Monitoring System and in other areas.

6. Acknowledgment

We wish to thank the DICE team for their support and feedback. We also thank T. Kachelhoffer and P-Y. Jallud for their contribution on the Adonis project and Yonny Cardenas for his contribution on TIDRA project.

7. References

http://cc.in2p3.fr/
http://dicom.offis.de/dcmtk.php.en
http://www.esrf.eu/
http://www.tge-adonis.fr/
http://www.cines.fr/
http://www.fedora-commons.org/
http://www.lsst.org/lsst
http://doublechooz.in2p3.fr/Public/public.php
https://forge.in2p3.fr/wiki/jux
http://wiki.arcs.org.au/bin/view/Main/HermeS
http://staff.science.uva.nl/~ptdeboer/vbrowser/
http://grid.in2p3.fr/jsaga/
http://www.slac.stanford.edu/BFROOT/
http://www.bioemergences.eu/
http://snfactory.lbl.gov/

Using iRODS to Preserve and Publish a Dataverse Archive

Mason Chua*, Antoine de Torcy**, Jewel H. Ward***, Jonathan Crabtree*
*H.W. Odum Institute for Research in Social Science
** Data Intensive Cyber Environments Center
*** School of Information and Library Science
The University of North Carolina at Chapel Hill

Abstract

We developed a method for transferring the contents of an archive running Dataverse, a publishing program for scientific data, into iRODS [5]. This method respects the encapsulation of the Dataverse archive by exporting its contents through documented methods using the OAI-PMH and HTTP protocols. Since the metadata exported from Dataverse conforms to documented standards (including the OAI-PMH and at least one other metadata specification), we were able to use an XSL transformation to reformat it into a document whose contents can be deserialized into the iRODS metadata catalog. As a result, iRODS users can use iRODS metadata to do keyword searches on the serialized copy of the Dataverse archive. Furthermore, this method lets administrators use iRODS to apply data preservation policies, including storage resource redundancy, to the contents of a Dataverse archive.

Index Keyword Terms—OAI-PMH, DDI, data archive, digital library, descriptive metadata, preservation, web publishing, migration, interoperability, XML, XSL transformation, serializa–tion, HTTP, search.

1. Introduction

The archivists at the H. W. Odum Institute for Research in Social Science use an open-source web publishing platform called Dataverse to publish their extensive collection of files related to social science research studies. As part of the Odum Institute's effort to test interoperability between archive platforms and data grid technologies, we developed a method to automatically copy the contents of a Dataverse archive into iRODS. The result is an accurate copy of a Dataverse archive inside iRODS, which data grid administrators can preserve over the long term by, for example, replicating the information to many geographically distributed storage resources. The transfer process also automatically populates the iRODS metadata catalog with descriptions of the data. This descriptive metadata lets iRODS users search the archive much as Dataverse users can do keyword searches using the web.

This paper assumes no knowledge of Dataverse, whose relevant features are explained in the following section. We do, however, assume a basic understanding of iRODS,

as explained in chapter 2 of the iRODS Primer [3]. Section 2.2 explains the relevant differences between Dataverse and iRODS, and Section 3 describes how we overcome these differences in order to automatically transfer a Dataverse archive into iRODS. Section 4 explains the significance of this work.

title World urbanization, 1950-1970
handle hdl:1902.29/D-488
distributor Odum Institute Dataverse Network
citation Davis, Kingsley, 1970, ''World Urbanization, 1950-1970'', http://hdl.handle.net/1902.29/D-488, Odum Institute [Distributor]
holdings URI http://arc/study?globalId=hdl:1902.29/D-488

Figure 1: On the Dataverse website, metadata is displayed as human-readable attribute-value pairs, hiding the underlying hierarchical structure (as seen in figure 2).

2. Background

2.1. The source: Dataverse

Dataverse is a publishing program for data archives. From the user's point of view, it is a web library of files associated with metadata.

```
<record>
<metadata>
   <docDscr>
      <citation>
         <titlStmt>
            <titl>World urbanization, 1950-1970</titl>
            <IDNo agency="handle">hdl:1902.29/D-488</IDNo>
         </titlStmt>
         <distStmt>
            <distrbtr>Odum Institute Dataverse Network</distrbtr>
            <distDate date="2007-11-30">2007-11-30</distDate>
         </distStmt>
         <biblCit format="DVN">
            Davis, Kingsley, 1970, "World urbanization, 1950-1970",
         <distStmt>
            <distrbtr>Odum Institute Dataverse Network</distrbtr>
            <distDate date="2007-11-30">2007-11-30</distDate>
         </distStmt>
         <biblCit format="DVN">
            Davis, Kingsley, 1970, "World urbanization, 1950-1970",
            http://hdl.handle.net/1902.29/D-488,
            Odum Institute [Distributor]
         </biblCit>
```

```
    <holdingsURI="http://arc/study?globalId=hdl:1902.29/D-488"/>
      </citation>
    </docDscr>
  </metadata>
</record>
```

Figure 2: An excerpt of the serialized version
of a typical metadata object in Dataverse.

For example, a file that contains the numerical results of a survey would be paired with metadata that contains the survey's location, description, location, sample size, date range, keywords, citation requirements, and even the contents of the survey questions. Researchers can find files on Dataverse by requesting keyword searches of the metadata.

Under the hood, Dataverse stores its information in a filesystem directory and a relational database, which are both hidden from the users. It is technically possible to back up an entire Dataverse archive by just copying these underlying files and database tables. These **raw backups** are risky, however, because their format might not be compatible with future versions of Dataverse. Although a raw backup contains all of the information in the digital library, recreating an archive from the backup might require inventing an ad hoc conversion process between formats. To prevent this problem, the Dataverse developers have provided two standard interfaces for exporting information from the library: the metadata can be downloaded using the OAI-PMH protocol, and (as mentioned above) the files can be downloaded through the HTTP protocol. OAI-PMH is a protocol for metadata harvesting that transfers XML over HTTP [2]. Although the metadata on a Dataverse website looks like a flat association list, such as the one below, its internal structure can conform to one of many existing metadata standards, including USMARC, Dublin Core, and DDI [1, 4].

The methods described in this paper can be applied to any of the metadata formats that Dataverse can export, but the particular examples are designed for DDI metadata. This metadata is a tree structure serialized as an XML document, like all metadata transferred through OAI-PMH.

2.2. The destination: iRODS

In iRODS, each metadata element is a list of three strings, called the **attribute**, **value**, and **unit**, together called an **AVU**. iRODS users can associate any AVU with any file in the iRODS data grid (assuming they have permission to do so).

Like Dataverse, iRODS can perform keyword searches by generating lists of objects whose metadata match arbitrary string expressions. But unlike Dataverse, iRODS does not store any hierarchical structure on the set of metadata elements associated with a file. Compare the serialized iRODS metadata in figure 3 to the serialized Dataverse metadata in figure 2: in Dataverse, a file's metadata is a hierarchical tree of metadata elements that

can have arbitrary text fields associated with them, An iRODS file's metadata, in contrast, is an unstructured set of AVUs. The main challenge of this project is finding a way to use iRODS to both preserve the hierarchical structure of the metadata in a Dataverse archive while exposing its contents to iRODS features, such as keyword searching.

3. Methods

We split the goal of this project into two parts and addressed each one separately.

3.1. Part one: Preservation

iRODS's ability to preserve data is a result of its abstraction of storage: each data object can be reduntantly stored in many geographically separated machines. Therefore, for the sake of preservation, it makes sense to serialize the contents of a Dataverse archive and then store them as data objects in iRODS, exposing them to the replication and integrity-checking features of iRODS.

Our automatic transfer script, called **Dataverse-to-iRODS**, takes advantage of Dataverse's ability to export serialized versions of its files and metadata through the HTTP and OAI-PMH protocols (respectively). The transfer of data objects depends on the transfer of metadata, because each metadata object contains URL references to the files it describes. After Dataverse-to-iRODS has run, iRODS has a collection containing each XML metadata object and the files it refers to. Here are the steps of the transfer process:

1. Dataverse-to-iRODS uses OAI-PMH to request a list of identifiers, which are the unique names of the metadata objects in the Dataverse.
2. The list of identifiers is an XML document. Dataverse-to-iRODS uses SAX to extract each identifier and use it to request a metadata object through OAI-PMH.
3. Each metadata object is an XML document. Dataverse-to-iRODS uploads the XML document into an iRODS collection corresponding to its identifier.
4. For each metadata object, Dataverse-to-iRODS also uses SAX again to extract the URL of each data object that the metadata refers to. It then downloads each object by HTTP and uploads it into the same collection as the metadata that refers to it.

As seen in steps 2 and 4, it is the metadata itself that lets Dataverse-to-iRODS discover the URLs of data objects and identifiers of other metadata objects. This discovery process is only possible because the metadata conforms to well-documented standards. The initial list of metadata identifiers conforms to the OAI-PMH protocol, which allowed us to write the XML parser that extracts each identifier. Similarly, each metadata object itself conforms to the DDI standard, which specifies the contents and hierarchy of the metadata precisely enough that we can parse out the URL of every file that the metadata refers to.

3.2. Part two: Exposure

We wanted the contents of Dataverse archives to be as accessible to iRODS users as possible. Dataverse websites let users browse for studies categorically and find them by keyword searches. In this project, we used iRODS's metadata catalog to re-implement these keyword search capabilities over a Dataverse archive after it has been serialized and transferred into iRODS. For each XML document containing Dataverse metadata, we automatically use its contents to compute the producer, notes, topic classification, explicitly-listed keywords, and about ten other fields that pertain to the metadata and its related files. We then ingest these fields into the iRODS metadata catalog and associate them with both the XML file containing the original metadata and the data objects that the metadata refers to. As a result, iRODS users can use the iquest program to perform the same keyword searches that are available through Dataverse. For example, the following command, when typed on one line, will return a list of iRODS collections containing all objects whose distributor contains the string "Odum Institute".

```
iquest "SELECT DATA NAME, COLL NAME
where META DATA ATTR NAME like
    '%Study Distributor'
and META DATA ATTR VALUE like
    '%Odum Institute%' "
```

Since the iquest program allows arbitrary metadata queries, it is not as user-friendly as Dataverse for basic keyword searches. It would be easy, however, to recreate Datavere's ease of searching by writing a web interface that translates the contents of an intuitive web form into an iquest query.

This metadata ingest process occurs automatically during each Dataverse-to-iRODS transfer, with the following steps:

1. After uploading each XML document containing metadata, Dataverse-to-iRODS calls an iRODS rule.
2. The iRODS rule calls the msiXSLTransformationApply microservice, which applies an XSL Transformation to the XML-encoded metadata to extracts the parts of the metadata that we think users will want to search for by keyword.
3. The rule writes the resulting transformed XML to a temporary file. This transformed XML is a list of attribute, value and unit triples.

```
<metadata>
    <AVU>
        <Attribute>title</Attribute>
        <Value>World urbanization, 1950-1970</Value>
        <Unit></Unit>
```

```
    </AVU>
    <AVU>
        <Attribute>handle</Attribute>
        <Value>hdl:1902.29/D-488</Value>
        <Unit></Unit>
    </AVU>
    <AVU>
        <Attribute>distributor</Attribute>
        <Value>Odum Institute Dataverse Network</Value>
        <Unit></Unit>
    </AVU>
</metadata>
```

Figure 3: A serialized set of iRODS metadata objects attached to a single file. The "attribute, value, unit" triples are not arranged in any hierarchical structure, except for being attached to the same file.

4. The rule calls the msiLoadMetadataFromXml microservice, which ingests these AVUs into the iRODS metadata catalog.
5. The rule associates the AVUs with each object that they apply to – the XML file containing the metadata that the AVUs were derived from, as well as the data files that the metadata refers to.

Although each AVU can be attached to many files, the iRODS metadata system only stores one copy of it in its internal database.

As in section 3.1, the success of this process relies on the fact that Dataverse and iRODS conform to documented standards. Because Dataverse's exported metadata conforms to both OAI-PMH as well as the DDI specification, it was possible to write the XSL Transformation that extracts the parts of the metadata that we wanted iRODS users to be able to search for. The metadata ingest also exploits iRODS's ability to both perform XSL transformations and deserialize an XML list of AVUs into the metadata catalog.

4. Conclusions

This paper has described how our script, Dataverse-to-iRODS, automatically creates a copy of a Dataverse archive inside iRODS, exposing it to iRODS's long-term preservation mechanisms and metadata-based search features. Dataverse-to-iRODS uses existing standards, namely OAI-PMH, XML, and any OAI-PMH-compatible metadata specification, to copy the data into iRODS data objects for preservation and ingest selected metadata fields into the metadata catalog to allow for keyword searching.

5. References

[1] Gary King, Merce Crosas, Ellen Kraffmiller, Leonid Andreev, Gustavo Durand, Robert Treacy, Kevin Condon, Michael Heppler, and Akio Sone. The Dataverse Network Project/Features. Retrieved Februrary 26, 2010, from http://thedata.org/software/features.

[2] Carl Lagoze and Herbert Van de Sompel. The open archives initiative: building a low-barrier interoperability framework. In *ACM/IEEE Joint Conference on Digital Libraries*, pages 54–62, 2001.

[3] Arcot Rajasekar, Michael Wan, Reagan Moore, Wayne Schroeder, Sheau-Yen Chen, Lucas Gilbert, Chien-Yi Hou, Christopher A. Lee, Richard Marciano, Paul Tooby, Antoine de Torcy, and Bing Zhu. *iRODS Primer*. Synthesis Lectures on Information Concepts, Retrieval, and Services. Morgan & Claypool Publishers, 2010.

[4] Mary Vardigan, Pascal Heus, and Wendey Thomas. Data Documentation Initiative: Toward a Standard for the Social Sciences. *The International Journal of Digital Curation*, 3(1), 2008.

[5] Jewel H. Ward, Antoine de Torcy, Mason Chua, and Jonathan Crabtree. Extracting and Ingesting DDI Metadata and Digital Objects from a Data Archive into the iRODS extension of the NARA TPAP using the OAI-PMH. In the *5th IEEE International Conference on e-Science*, Oxford, UK, December 2009.

Conceptualizing Policy-Driven Repository Interoperability (PoDRI) Using iRODS and Fedora

David Pcolar
Carolina Digital Repository (CDR)
UNC Chapel Hill
david_pcolar@unc.edu

Daniel W. Davis
Cornell Information Sciences (CIS)
DuraSpace Affiliate
dwdavis@cs.cornell.edu

Bing Zhu
Data Intensive Cyber Environments
University of California: San Diego
bizhu@ucsd.edu

Alexandra Chassanoff
School of Information & Library
Science (SILS)
UNC Chapel Hill
achass@email.unc.edu

Chien-Yi Hou
Sustainable Archives & Leveraging
Technologies (SALT)
UNC Chapel Hill
chienyi@unc.edu

Richard Marciano
Sustainable Archives & Leveraging
Technologies (SALT)
UNC Chapel Hill
richard_marciano@unc.edu

Abstract

Given the growing need for cross-repository integration to enable a trusted, scalable, open and distributed content infrastructure, this paper introduces the Policy-Driven Repository Interoperability (PoDRI) project investigating interoperability mechanisms between repositories at the policy level. Simply moving digital content from one repository to another may not capture the essential management policies needed to ensure its integrity and authenticity. This project is focused on integrating policy-aware object models, including policy expressions, and a distributed architecture for policy-driven management, demonstrated using iRODS and Fedora as representative open source software products. Using iRODS and its Rules engine, combined with Fedora's rich semantic object model for digital objects, enables use of the best features of both products.

Index Keyword Terms—iRODS, Fedora, Preservation, Policy Management

1. Introduction

This paper introduces the Policy-Driven Repository Interoperability (PoDRI) project, investigating inter–operability between repositories at the policy level. PoDRI is led by the University of North Carolina at UNC, with units ranging from SALT (Sustainable Archives & Leveraging Technologies), RENCI (Renaissance Computing Institute), SILS (School of Information and Library Science), and the Libraries/CDR (Carolina Digital Repository). Key partners include Bing Zhu at UCSD (DICE, Data Intensive Cyber Environments) and Daniel Davis at DuraSpace (combining DSpace and Fedora Commons) and Cornell Information Sciences. The project is sponsored by an Institute of Museum and Library Services (IMLS) National Leadership grant and is motivated by the growing need to create a scalable, open, and distributed infrastructure that provides durable, trusted access and management of our valuable digital content of all kinds (e.g. research data sets, documents, video, metadata).

Simply replicating digital content from one repository, with or without any associated metadata, may not capture the essential management policies that ensure integrity and authenticity, a critical requirement for establishing a trust model. "A policy is typically a rule describing the interactions of actions that take place within the archive, or a constraint determining when and by whom an action may be taken." [1]. A distributed policy management architecture is an essential component in realizing a trust mechanism for repository interoperability. The PoDRI project investigates the requirements for policy-aware interoperability and demonstrates key features needed for its implementation. The project is focused on integrating object models, including interoperable policy expressions, and a policy-aware distributed architecture that includes both repositories and middleware services.

The PoDRI project addresses the following research problem: **What is the feasibility of repository interoperability at the policy level?** Research questions to be addressed are:

- Can a preservation environment be assembled from two existing repositories?
- Can the policies of the federation be enforced across repositories?
- Can policies be migrated between repositories?
- What fundamental mechanisms are needed within a repository to implement new policies?

iRODS, the Integrated Rule-Oriented Data System [2, 3] and the Fedora Repository [4, 5] will be used as representative open source software to demonstrate the PoDRI architecture. Combining iRODS and Fedora enables use of the best features of both products for building sustainable digital repositories. iRODS provides an integrated rule engine, distributed virtual storage, the iCAT (iRODS Metadata Catalog)[1], and Micro-services[2]. Fedora offers a rich semantic object modeling for digital objects, extensible format-neutral metadata and a flexible service mediation mechanism.

2. Rationale for Integrating Fedora and iRODS

Early in 2006, the DART [6] project created an Storage Resource Broker (SRB) storage interface for Fedora that allows all Fedora digital content, including Fedora Digital Objects (FDO) and their Datastreams, to be stored in SRB distributed repositories. Similarly, a storage module was developed by Aschenbrenner and Zhu [7] for iRODS. Using the Fedora-iRODS storage module, iRODS can act as a back-end for Fedora, and thus provide opportunities for Fedora to use iRODS capabilities such as virtual federated storage, micro-services and the rules engine.

iRODS offers an appealing platform for implementing a distributed policy-driven management architecture. The integrated rules engine can be used to invoke a range of rules including policy expressions and, through the use of micro-services, can execute code for those policies in a distributed environment. Rules can act as simple workflows, performing a sequence of pre-defined actions. iRODS rules can be executed explicitly, triggered by external conditions or events, and executed at timed intervals. For example, iRODS can implement a replication policy, geographically disbursing file copies across the network. Micro-services can be written for feature extraction, format migration, integrity checks and other preservation services.

While used to efficiently hold and query structured data and metadata, the iCAT relational database is not optimal for handling the complex, variable metadata needed for preservation and curation. Indeed, any relational database will require considerable coding to support complex metadata schemas, making the use of unstructured data (files) possibly in combination with XML databases or semantic triplestores a more flexible alternative [8].

Fedora is file-centric; all Fedora data and metadata is stored in files [9]. The Fedora Digital Object (FDO), a kind of compound digital object, provides the organizing metadata used to "make sense" of itself and other resources. It uses the FOXML schema to encapsulate metadata, and to reference other files or web resources. Since the FDO is a file, it can be stored in iRODS like any other file.

Digital content (or user-defined metadata) managed by the FDO is stored in one or more separate files – each registered in a FOXML element called a Datastream. Datastreams can also capture relationships to other objects and external resources. Users may add metadata to the FDO or add additional metadata Datastreams (to be stored like any other file.

This means, however, that metadata is stored in an unstructured, often XML or RDF way, and requires external indices to support queries such as search engines, semantic triplestores, XML databases, and now the iCAT. Fedora's approach provides a format-neutral, extensible framework for representing data and metadata.

The rich metadata environment provided by the FDO can augment the structured metadata found in the iCAT. Metadata can be copied from the iCAT into a more easily preserved unstructured file format, as demonstrated by Bing Zhu and colleagues [10]. Critical data can be copied from the FDO, or as user metadata files (Datastreams), so they can be queried from the iCAT. With suitable metadata, both the iCAT and Fedora could be entirely rebuilt from files if the indices were lost or corrupted.

Fedora has a set of "front-end" APIs that provide the means to ingest and manipulate FDOs (CRUD). iRODS is capable of calling these APIs to perform operations from micro-services. Fedora also provides an extensible mechanism to add custom functionality called "services" that are executed within the context of the FDO. Services act as extensions to the "front-end" API of the object. Fedora mediates the service request calling the appropriate "back-end" functionality. The back-end functionality can be a Web service, in this case potentially provided by iRODS. Custom Fedora services provide another mechanism to interact with iRODS. Since iRODS can interact with Fedora's "front-end" APIs, "back-end" services, and the Fedora-iRODS storage module one may picture iRODS wrapping around Fedora.

3. First Steps Toward a Policy-driven Management Architecture

To demonstrate distributed policy-driven manage–ment architecture, we plan to implement the following operational scenarios:

- Integrate views of content, original arrangement (hierarchy) and metadata
- Create an audit trail of policy execution events and related provenance information
- Manage policies through Fedora
- Show iRODS invoking policies from Fedora

Both iRODS and Fedora fully support distributed computing installations. In effect, both products can be

---

[1] iCAT is the iRODS Metadata Catalog that stores metadata about all objects in iRODS in a relational database.

[2] Micro-services are function snippets or executables that can be used to perform a distinct task using well-defined input information structures.

characterized as virtualization middleware for storage, access, and service execution. The products, however, have very different operational paradigms which must be accommodated, but provide complementary strengths that can be exploited when used together.

The virtual file system in iRODS makes it the logical choice for all storage (including FDOs). In addition, the iRODS rules engine and micro-services provide an effective means for policy invocation. Fedora's capabilities are especially powerful for handling variable content and metadata formats, to flexibly relate resources, to facilitate presentation, and its mediation capabilities make it appealing for supporting systems that are "designed for change."

A policy-driven management architecture requires that policy expressions be persistent somewhere. Fedora could be used to create FDOs containing policy expressions, which are subsequently loaded into actionable form and invoked in iRODS. As policies are part of the provenance, Fedora can relate the policy FDOs to the content items to which they apply. Since policy invocation is performed by iRODS, audit records of the execution must be created by iRODS; this will likely be done by creating FDOs (and relating them to the FDOs containing the content and policy expressions).

iRODS does not currently generate audit data in a format compliant with the PREMIS schema. The CDR implements auditing of objects via a PREMIS.XML file for each iRODS data object. This method may not be sustainable for repositories containing millions of objects. Preservation activities, such as replication or fixity checks, generate large amounts of log entries over time and potentially exceed the byte size of the original object. Discussions between CDR and iRODS developers suggest multiple methods for retaining and aggregating various component logs for translation into PREMIS-compliant events. Do we continue to store these events with the individual objects or as an aggregate? Do we generate specific PREMIS information upon request? In the case of replicas residing on disparate nodes in a data grid, auditable events will occur that differ from those affecting the original object. How do we reconcile these events in a singular view of the object?

Users and user applications will still need to interact with Fedora or iRODS directly. This is particularly true of research (grid) applications having large datasets. Selected metadata will need to be duplicated in both products to access content, represent arrangements, and preserve integrity and authenticity. Direct interaction by users or user applications with either Fedora or iRODS might require both products to synchronize or update metadata.

These interactions may trigger policy invocations. For example, Fedora may trigger policy invocation indirectly when interacting with a file (CRUD) or directly through a Fedora custom service. Conversely, iRODS' micro-services can call Fedora services to provide feedback in the system.

A more comprehensive "Concept of Operations" document will be prepared as part of the PoDRI project. The following set of questions is drawn from our current understanding of the operational scenarios:

- How will the collection structure be represented in the two products?
- How will Fedora be initialized for existing content in iRODS?
- How will Fedora be informed of content or metadata changes initiated directly in iRODS?
- How can content or metadata from Fedora be accessed by iRODS services?

4. Enabling Use Cases

Five enabling use cases have been identified for the Fedora-iRODS integration. These use cases are:

1. New content ingest via Fedora
2. New content ingest via iRODS
3. Bulk registration from iRODS into Fedora
4. Update of content or metadata via Fedora
5. Update of content or metadata via iRODS

We describe the first two use cases in this paper; a full discussion of all the use cases is beyond the scope of this paper, and will be developed and documented throughout the project's lifecycle. While these use cases do not, by themselves represent policy management operations, they are prerequisites for enabling policy-driven operations and represent demonstrations of policy interoperability between repositories.

4.1 New Content Ingest via Fedora

Current users of Fedora will want to continue ingesting into Fedora. Users are also likely to use Fedora features to add and relate rich metadata including policy, provenance and authenticity information. As shown in Figure 1, when new content is ingested into Fedora, it is able to capture the metadata it needs for its operation. Digital content (or user-defined metadata) is either pulled in by Fedora or pushed to Fedora and stored in individual files. The file containing the FDO (FOXML) and the content files are subsequently stored in iRODS with no storage directly managed by Fedora.

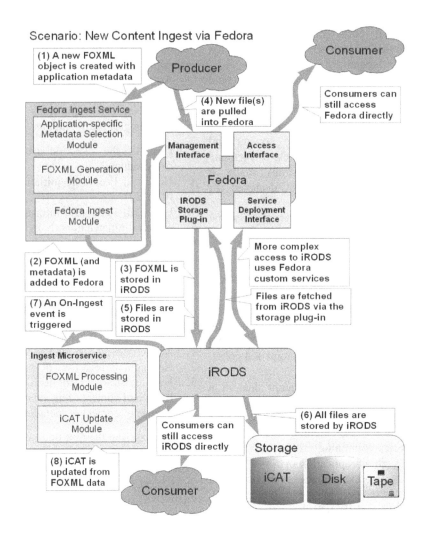

Figure 5: New Content Ingest via Fedora

Selected metadata is collected by Fedora during the ingest process and stored in an internal system index implemented using a relational database. This database is used only to remove latency (speed up) access to content or bindings to services (formerly called disseminators). Optionally, metadata or notifications can be sent to index services such as semantic triplestores, search engines and OAI-PMH harvesters.

The Carolina Digital Repository (CDR) is using Solr/Lucene as the indexing and search engine for discovery of ingested content. Metadata is extracted during the ingest process from MODS and FOXML files.

Objects ingested via Fedora and stored in iRODS do not, by default, retain the logical tree structure of the original file system. Instead, CDR preserves the hierarchal structure of the file system via relations in the RDF triple store.

The arrangement of objects is achieved by created FDOs representing the parent and child. The relationship is recorded in RDF (within the RELS-EXT Datastream) using the "isMemberOf" asserted in the child to the parent. The obverse relation "hasMember" is implied but could be stated explicitly in the parent. These two relations provide a way to build a hierarchical structure for all objects, collections and files. In Fedora, these relations form a "graph" and objects may participate in any number of graphs using other relations and, therefore, are not limited to a single hierarchy. Relationship information can be accessed by introspecting on the FDO or the relations can be indexed into a RDF triplestore [11] and queried by applications to extract a graph for navigating from parent to children as people usually do for a tree structure. Similar methods can be used to navigate any relationship graph.

How will the metadata in iRODS be updated in this use case? Two alternatives being considered are: (1) call a

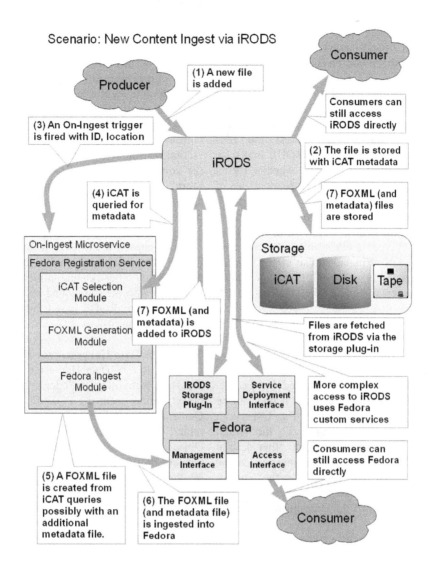

Scenario: New Content Ingest via iRODS

Producer

(1) A new file is added

Consumer

Consumers can still access iRODS directly

(3) An On-Ingest trigger is fired with ID, location

iRODS

(2) The file is stored with iCAT metadata

(4) iCAT is queried for metadata

(7) FOXML (and metadata) files are stored

On-Ingest Microservice

Fedora Registration Service

iCAT Selection Module

FOXML Generation Module

Fedora Ingest Module

(7) FOXML (and metadata) is added to iRODS

Storage

iCAT | Disk | Tape

Files are fetched from iRODS via the storage plug-in

IRODS Storage Plug-In | Service Deployment Interface

More complex access to iRODS uses Fedora custom services

Fedora

Management Interface | Access Interface

Consumers can still access Fedora directly

(5) A FOXML file is created from iCAT queries possibly with an additional metadata file.

(6) The FOXML file (and metadata file) is ingested into Fedora

Consumer

Figure 6: New Content Ingest via iRODS

Fedora custom service to update the iCAT; (2) when the FOXML file is ingested, a monitoring rule can trigger an iRODS micro-service to introspect on the FDO to extract the metadata.

4.2 New Content Ingest via iRODS

Current iRODS users will likely want to continue to use iRODS directly to store data objects, particularly in research settings where direct access to storage is desired. The digital content (data object) is typically ingested into iRODS as a file operation. In iRODS, the hierarchical relation of a data object and its ancestors are encoded and described explicitly in its global object name. Two questions arise from this scenario. First, how will Fedora be notified of arrival of the new data object? Second, how

will an analog to its iRODS hierarchy be represented in Fedora?

A utility is needed to register iRODS files into Fedora. A micro-service could call this utility when triggered by a monitoring rule on the storage operation which would create the FDO for the data object and ingest it into Fedora. The micro-service can be deployed as a rule under the iRODS rule event, 'acPostProcForPut'. Once this rule is activated in an iRODS server, the micro-service can be triggered after each new iRODS data object is created in a specified collection in the iRODS Content Store (see iRODS Storage Module), as depicted in Figure 2. It will create pre-ingest FOXML for the new data object, querying the iCAT for additional metadata as needed. Within the FOXML, it will create a Datastream containing a reference to the location of the data object within iRODS. It will then ingest the FOXML using Fedora's API-M to create the FDO. This rule is activated once placed in the rule configuration file of an iRODS server. It monitors all file activities in the iCAT catalog and creates an FDO for any newly created iRODS file.

When using iRODS for back-end storage, all FDOs and Datastreams are stored in iRODS as files in one of two collections: FOXML Object Store and iRODS Content Store. Therefore, users can directly access the files containing Fedora metadata through the iRODS interface. On the other hand, files stored in iRODS, whether for an FDO or a Datastream, have both an independent set of iRODS system metadata as well as a set of user-defined metadata. The system metadata contains important information for each replica of an iRODS file, including the file's location, storage type, audit trail, and associated iRODS rules. The two sets of metadata can be represented as external Datastreams in FOXML and generated dynamically when accessed using the Fedora-iRODS storage module.

As described above, Fedora uses RDF relations to describe the arrangement of objects. This requires the creation of FDOs representing each hierarchical level which has the advantage of enabling the participation of iRODS in the semantic network functionality provided by Fedora. Since iRODS can create a virtual hierarchy, it may not be desirable to instantiate corresponding FDOs. Users can create custom Datastreams as "finding aids"; the virtual hierarchy can be encoded using RDF or any other desired format. Similar to iRODS, parent-child relationships can be modeled as path metadata and stored in the custom Datastream. An application or a Fedora custom service can be used to interpret the format of the Datastream to display the hierarchy [12].

Many of the CDR's core constituencies are the special collections in our libraries. These collections tend to have rich metadata associated with them and have usually undergone preliminary curation. The longer term goal of the repository is to harvest content directly from research-based iRODS data grids. Metadata quality and quantity is typically limited in these collections. Repository outreach and development is concerned not only with identifying and preserving "at risk" collections, but cultivating metadata collection and data curation proactively throughout the research lifecycle.

5. Additional Utilities

We plan to implement two utilities in addition to the functionality described above. First is an updated storage module as an iRODS-specific plug-in to replace Fedora's Low-level Store. Second is a harvester utility which can be used in both bulk registration and for disaster recovery.

5.1 iRODS Storage Module

We plan to store all files in iRODS. This will require an update of the existing iRODS-Fedora Storage Module or build a new module potentially using the Fedora Commons Akubra interface. If a new module is built, using Jargon is being considered. Building a new module would permit research on using it as a feedback path for policy operations including security policies.

When iRODS serves as a storage module for Fedora, current thought is to use two iRODS collections: (1) Fedora Digital Objects (FOXML) in the FOXML Object Store, and (2) content objects (Datastreams) in the iRODS Content Store. They are accessed through a single curator user account in iRODS. This makes it easier to distinguish between policies related to FDOs from those operating on content objects (Datastreams).

This approach, however, differs from the Fedora/Jargon default of storing objects in folders based on timestamp. For the CDR and other existing implementations, a restructuring of objects into the segregated object store will be required. This will alter iRODS based failure recovery mechanisms and integrity audits.

5.2 iRODS Data Harvester for Fedora

The iRODS Data Harvester is an adaptive version of the Data Rebuilder in Fedora. It is used to re-build the object indices from the FOXML Object Store and iRODS Content Store. It does not create any new FOXML objects; rather, it surveys all the objects stored within the FOXML Object Store, verifies the Datastreams inside the iRODS Content Store, and creates the indices in the database used by the Fedora server. The iRODS Data Harvester also builds the necessary RDF data to be stored in the RDF triplestore for the navigation of hierarchical structure.

6. Policy Federation and Migration

The iRODS rule engine provides the capability to apply rules on the data grid side to implement the policies. The Distributed Custodial Archival Preservation Environments (DCAPE) project [13] aims to work with a group of archivists to develop a set of rules to automate many of the administrative tasks associated with the management of archival repositories and validation of their trustworthiness. These DCAPE rules could be applied to different repositories based on the institution's policies. We plan to provide the functionality for users to manage the policies through the Fedora interface and be able to check what rules are in action.

Current implementations, even in data grid environments, depend on local enforcement of policies and typically do not consider the larger framework of uniform policy implementation across heterogeneous repositories. If policies are expressed in the language of ISO-MOIMS or DCAPE criteria, we have a clear model for identification of machine-actionable rules.

Stored as Fedora Service Definitions, the policies will have unique service deployment bindings for each data storage system. Our demonstration storage implementation is iRODS, but other storage environments may be supported by changing deployment mechanisms.

The CDR is developing a policy management framework based on a machine interpretable series of actions across repositories in a data grid. Implementation of new policy requires identification of machine- actionable components and mapping to specific, testable deployment mechanisms.

7. Summary

In this paper, we introduced the Policy-Driven Repository Interoperability (PoDRI) project investigating interoperability mechanisms between repositories at the policy level. The rationale for using iRODS and Fedora to demonstrate key features of a distributed policy-driven management architecture was described. Four scenarios that will be demonstrated as part of the project were enumerated. We have identified five enabling use cases and described two that are needed for the demonstration scenarios along with two key utilities planned for development. We also introduced work on policy federation and migration. PoDRI is an applied research project and its details will change as we develop a greater understanding of the methods for policy-driven interoperability.

8. Acknowledgements

This project is funded by IMLS grant LG-06-09-0184-09 as part of the 2009 National Leadership Grants NLG Library-Research and Demonstration, awarded to the University of North Carolina at Chapel Hill. Project Director is Richard Marciano. Collaborators at UNC / SILS include: Alex Chassanoff, Chien-Yi Hou, Reagan Moore, and Helen Tibbo. At UNC / Libraries: Steve Barr, Greg Jansen, Will Owen, and Dave Pcolar. At UNC / RENCI: Leesa Brieger. At UCSD: Bing Zhu. At DuraSpace and Cornell Information Sciences: Daniel Davis and Sandy Payette. Finally, at the University of Maryland iSchool: Bruce Ambacher.

9. References

[1] DuraSpace, "PLEDGE Project," http://fedora-commons.org/confluence/x/WSDS

[2] iRODS: Data Grids, Digital Libraries, Persistent Archives, and Real-time Data Systems. http://www.irods.org

[3] R. Moore, A. Rajasekar, M. Wan, and W. Schroeder, "Policy-Based Distributed Data Management Systems," The 4th International Conference on Open Repositories, Atlanta, Georgia, May 19, 2009.

[4] Fedora Commons, http://www.fedora-commons.org

[5] Fedora Commons, "Fedora Repository Documentation," http://fedora-commons.org/confluence/x/AgAU

[6] DART, University of Queensland, "Fedora-SRB Database integration module," http://www.itee.uq.edu.au/~eresearch/projects/dart/outcomes/FedoraDB.php

[7] A. Aschenbrenner, B. Zhu, iRODS, "iRODS-Fedora Integration," http://www.irods.org/index.php/Fedora

[8] M. Hedges, A. Hazan, and T. Blanke, "Management and Preservation of Research Data with iRODS," *Proceedings of the ACM first workshop on CyberInfrastructure: information management in eScience*, Lisbon, Portugal, pp. 17-22, 2007 doi: http://doi.acm.org/10.1145/1317353.1317358

[9] DuraSpace, "The Fedora Digital Object Model," http://fedora-commons.org/confluence/x/dgBI

[10] B. Zhu, R. Marciano, and R. Moore, "Enabling Inter-repository Access Management between iRODS and Fedora," The 4th International Conference on Open Repositories, Atlanta, Georgia, May 19, 2009.

[11] Wikipedia, "Triplestore," http://en.wikipedia.org/wiki/Triplestore

[12] DuraSpace, "The Content Model Architecture," http://fedora-commons.org/confluence/x/gABI

[13] DCAPE, "Distributed Custodial Archival Preservation Environments", an NHPRC-funded project, http://dcape.org

Community-Driven Development of Preservation Services

Funded Project Staff listed in Red and Blue

INTEGRATION & BUS DEV

UNC
  SALT
    Richard Marciano
    Chien-Yi Hou
  CDR
    Dave Pcolar ++

POLICY / RULE DEV

West Virginia University
  Donald Adjeroh
  Frances Van Scoy

RENCI
  Leesa Brieger ++

DICE
  Michael Conway ++
  Reagan Moore
  Antoine de Torcy ++

UNC Libraries
  Steve Barr ++
  Greg Jansen ++

UNC Res. Comp. Svcs
  Bill Schulz ++

SILS Grad. Student team
  Heather Bowden ++
  Alex Chassanoff ++
  Christine Cheng ++
  William Miao ++
  Terrell Russell ++
  Jewel Ward ++

UNC CS Grad. Student team
  Tao Yu ++
  Hao Xu ++

STATE ARCHIVES & LIB

Michigan
  Caryn Wojcik
  Mark Harvey

North Carolina
  Kelly Eubank
  Jennifer Ricker ++
  Amy Rudersdorf ++
  Lisa Gregory ++
  Ed Southern --
  Megan Durden --
  IT
  Dean Farrell ++
  Druscie Simpson
  David Minor
  Chris Black --

Kentucky
  Glen McAninch
  Mark Myers ++

Kansas
  Scott Leonard

New York
  Bonnie Weddle
  Michael Martin ++
  Ann Marie Przybyla

California
  Chris Garmire
  Nancy Lenoil-Zimmelman
  Linda Johnson --
  Laren Metzer
  Renee Vincent-Finch --

UNIVERSITY ARCHIVES

Tufts University
  Eliot Wilczek
  Veronica Martzahl ++
  Anne Sauer

UNC Chapel Hill
  Will Owen ++
  Rich Szary ++

CULTURAL INSTITUTIONS

Getty Research Institute
  Joseph Shubitowski
  David Farneth
  Leah Prescott
  Sally Hubbard --
  Mahnaz Ghaznavi --
  Karim Boughida --

Smithsonian Institution Archives
  Riccardo Ferrante ++

SCHOOLS OF LIB & IS

UNC Chapel Hill
  Cal Lee ++

University of Wisconsin-Madison
  Kristin Eschenfelder ++

Legend	Collaborator Roles
Red	Funded
Blue	Cost-sharing
Brown	"Observer"
Black	None of the above
++	Added after project funded
--	At new institution

Abstract

This paper describes the first phase of the *DCAPE* project and the lessons learned in articulating a community-based development approach for preserva–tion services. The *"Distributed Custodial Archival Preservation Environments"* project, *DCAPE*, was funded by the National Historical Publications and Records Commission (NHPRC) in 2007, in a call for proposals for *"cooperative networks and service providers' projects."* The NHPRC's goal was to encourage the creation of e-records storage, preservation, and access services, and to promote sustainable business models. *DCAPE*'s approach proposed to develop a framework to support *institution-specific preservation policies* (including business models) while providing the economy of scale needed for a cost-effective service. The focus of this paper is on the community-driven nature of the preservation services development process.

Index Keyword Terms—Preservation Services, Trusted Digital Repositories, Policy Management, *DCAPE*, iRODS, SALT

1. Introduction

The goal of the *DCAPE* project is to build a distributed production preservation environment that meets the needs of mid-to-large-sized archival reposi–tories, libraries, and cultural institutions for trusted archival preservation services. The preservation environment builds upon the technologies developed at the University of North Carolina–Chapel Hill (UNC) Renaissance Computing Institute (RENCI) and the data storage infrastructure being installed there. The environment includes a trusted digital repository infrastructure that is assembled from a rule-based data management system, commodity storage systems, and sustainable preservation services. The software infrastructure automates many of the administrative tasks associated with management of archival repositories, including validation and trustworthiness.

Our proposal involves the collaboration of multiple "medium-scaled" preservation communities with the explicit goal of defining the common set of services needed by all participating institutions (state archives and libraries, university archives, cultural institutions, etc.), and the unique set of services that must be tuned to specific mandated policies at each site.

The original NHPRC grant called for the develop–ment of cooperative institutions to provide electronic records preservation services to repositories. A single award of up to $400K was to be made but in the end two awards were granted, one to the Emory-based MetaArchive project for $300K and another to the UNC-based *DCAPE* project for $258K.

- MetaArchive aims to develop a sustainable digital preservation service for cultural and historical records and a cost-model for providing preservation services based on the Lots of Copies Keep Stuff Safe (LOCKSS) model. In addition, the goal is to integrate LOCKSS with the Storage Resource Broker (SRB) and the Integrated Rule-Oriented Data System (iRODS) data grid technologies, developed by members of the DICE group at UNC Chapel Hill.
- *DCAPE* aims to develop a sustainable digital preservation service for state and university archives and other repositories, and a cost model for providing distributed and customized preservation services based on the iRODS model. The approach allows for the customization of services based on the profile of the archives or collections.

The innovative *DCAPE* approach intends to develop sets of machine-actionable preservation policies, but allow individual communities to customize the behaviors of these policies. Given the limited level of project funding, a collaborative and community-development approach has emerged, as demonstrated by the impressive list of participants and contributors in the project so far. The focus of this paper is on the community-driven nature of the preservation services development process.

2. A Sustainable Development Approach

Beyond the funded project staff, others have participated in conversations and meetings around the project., accounting for some 60 people! This is a reflection of *DCAPE*'s development philosophy of establishing a systematic and sustainable development partnership. We wish to reflect on several aspects of sustainability: (1) NHPRC's sustained investments in building collaborations, as demonstrated by the agency's funding agenda over the last twelve years, (2) the leveraging of community development when funds are limited, and (3) the sustainability of projects beyond the initial funding.

2.1 NHPRC's Sustained Funding in e-Records

NHPRC funded projects have been seminal in initiating and sustaining conversations between technologists and archivists over the last decade. Richard Marciano, principal investigator on *DCAPE*, has been privileged to participate in a series of NHPRC-funded projects starting in 2000 with the Archivists' Workbench.

		2000	2001	2002	2003	2004	2005	2006	2007	2008	2009	2010	2011
a.	Archivists' Workbench	▓	▓	▓									
b.	PERM			▓	▓	▓							
c.	ICAP					▓	▓	▓					
d.	PAT						▓	▓	▓				
e.	e-Legacy								▓	▓	▓		
f.	DCAPE										▓	▓	▓

Figure 1: NHPRC-funded projects leading to *DCAPE* at SDSC and UNC (Richard Marciano, PI)

DCAPE participants involved in these earlier projects include: Chien-Yi Hou (ICAP, PAT, e-Legacy), Reagan Moore (PAT, e-Legacy), Caryn Wojcik (Archivists' Workbench, PERM, PAT), Glen McAninch (PAT), Chris Garmire (e-Legacy), Nancy Lenoil-Zimmelman (e-Legacy), Linda Johnson (e-Legacy), Laren Metzer (e-Legacy), Renee Vincent-Finch (e-Legacy), Mahnaz Ghaznavi (PAT), and Karim Boughida (PAT).

The Archivists' Workbench (2000-02) was a three-year project conducted at the San Diego Supercomputer Center at the University of California, San Diego that focused on long-term preservation of and access to software-dependent electronic records. This project featured an archival advisory board consisting of many luminaries in the field: Ken Thibodeau (NARA), Theodore Hull (NARA), Bruce Ambacher (NARA), Phil Bantin (Indiana University), Charles Dollar (UBC), Pat Galloway (UT Austin), Anne Gilliland (UCLA), Peter Hirtle (Cornell), Heather MacNeil (UBC), Tom Ruller (NY State Archives), Lee Stout (Penn State), and Caryn Wojcik (State Archives of Michigan), with technical coordination by Mark Conrad (NARA) and Peter Bloniarz (SUNY at Albany). The input from these experts was significant and had a lasting impact.

Subsequently, the Preserving the Electronic Records Stored in an RMA (PERM) project (2002-04), with the State of Michigan, developed and tested a model for preserving electronic records stored in a records management application that complies with the Department of Defense (DoD) Standard 5015.2. The project evaluated the DoD Standard 5015.2 to determine which features of the RMA standard needed to be retained in any future preservation model.

The Incorporating Change Management into Archival Processes (ICAP) project with UCLA (2003-05), examined the issues involved in access to and long-term preservation of active electronic records that are being changed over time by their creators. Prototypes to study the versioning of records were developed.

The Persistent Archives Testbed (PAT) project (2004-07), was a precursor of *DCAPE*. PAT brought together four State Archives: the Michigan Historical Center, Minnesota Historical Society, Kentucky Department for Libraries and Archives, and Ohio Historical Society. The project explored data grid systems to handle large archival data sets and persistent archives technologies. The project made a case for distributed custody – where records remain in the system which created them while simultaneously being in archival custody.

Finally, the e-Legacy project (2007-10), which is still active, is developing hardware and software infrastructure to preserve the state's geospatial records created by the California Spatial Information Library and managed by the California State Archives.

In addition to these undertakings, Caryn Wojcik proposed development of commercial preservation service models (Preservation-as-a-Service). This idea and the earlier NHPRC-funded projects led to the collaborative network of technologists and archivists in *DCAPE*. These projects as well as many other previous NHPRC-funded projects of *DCAPE* participants, have helped bridge archival concepts and new technological advances. The *DCAPE* project builds on and contributes to this legacy of NHPRC supported conversations between archivists and technologists.

2.2 DCAPE's Community Development Approach

The goals of the *DCAPE* project are ambitious: (1) develop a set of policy and service definitions, driven by the requirements of the underlying partners; (2) implement these services; (3) test them with partner collections; and (4) develop business models for sustaining this effort. Also important – the *DCAPE* com–munity development of rule sets using iRODS is a first and sets the standard for other communities. Moreover, *DCAPE* must meet these challenges with limited resources. The NHPRC funding covers only 15% of one programmer. A subcontract with West Virginia University also allows summer time for a graduate student. Given these lofty goals and limited resources, a community-supported development model is key.

This community-driven development model accounts for the nearly 60 participants since the start of the project.

Some of the leveraging measures taken include (1) creating a new group called Sustainable Archives & Leveraging Technologies (SALT); (2) partnering with Dave Pcolar at UNC Libraries where the Carolina Digital Repository, UNC's institutional repository, is being developed; (3) establishing a policy/rule development discussion team that includes programmers from the Renaissance Computing Institute (RENCI), the Data Intensive Cyber Environments (DICE) group, UNC Libraries, UNC Research Computing Services, and graduate students from the School of Information and Library Science (SILS) and Computer Science (CS); and (4) assembling additional archivists, librarians, and IT staff from all six state archives and libraries; (5) new university archives – UNC Chapel Hill Libraries; (6) new cultural institutions – Smithsonian Institution's Archives; and (7) experts from two schools of information and library science.

This approach is fraught with challenges. Beyond the limitations of funding described above, there are management challenges associated with a virtual organization where input from individuals and groups is necessary, even as they are not accountable to the grant project. For example, collaborators have come and gone over the course of the project, as indicated by the "Collaborator Roles legend" on the first page. Collaboration with students and staff funded by other grants, but producing open-source software or other services for the *DCAPE* project, raises questions about grant time accounting and ownership of cooperatively created services. The cooperative model also complicates development of *DCAPE* service models and planning of actual management of the services.

2.3 Developing Sustainable Services

A number of business models are possible under the *DCAPE* approach, from hosting services, subscription mechanisms, membership fees, packaging rule sets as business intelligence, etc. We have partnered with UNC's Business School to explore a range of approaches. "Preservation-as-a-Service (PaaS) is a potential business model that may prove viable for *DCAPE*, as the technologies involved become commodities and the costs for significant amounts of storage fall." [1].

3. Development Methodology

Two core teams have been assembled: (1) a User Community Team, made up of the archivist and librarian partners; and (2) a Policy and Rule Development Team, made up of the NHPRC-funded staff developers, and also observers and teams of students from SILS and CS.

In the first six months of the project a Wiki was established. A working group from the User Community Team conducted an assessment of capabilities from the Reference Model for an Open Archival Information (OAIS) that are relevant to the project, based on requirements from their own institutions. This led to a specification with close to 100 policies. A working subset of 26 rules was extracted for pilot work. The team developed a research testbed SLA (service-level agreement) to facilitate loading of records from the partner institutions into a testbed. An assessment of the 26 pilot rules was conducted and related to CCSDS MOIMS-RAC Working Group's "Audit and Certification of Trustworthy Digital Repositories" draft standard that is currently being developed for submission to the International Organization for Standardization (ISO) [3]. The 26 rules were then expanded to 52, and these rules were mapped back to RAC rules (see Appendix 1).

In the second six months of the project, the Policy and Rule Development Team met weekly to interpret and map the 52 policies and map them into machine-actionable iRODS rules [2]. This team has implemented the rules using two instances of iRODS, a development testbed and a community testbed. Records from community members can be loaded according to the established SLA in the community testbed.

In the current phase of the project, both teams have come together face-to-face, and an integration team has been put together. The integration team will move to the next step of all the iRODS rules into the *DCAPE* implementations.

4. Summary

In this paper, we introduced the community-driven development methodology we are using to establish *DCAPE* preservation services. While community-development helps to overcome the deficiency of funding available for preservation projects, it also introduces complications in project management. As of early March 2010, we are at the half-way point. While much has been accomplished, much work remains. One significant accomplishment is the development of a set of community preservation rules – rules that are being created for the first time in the context of the project. The business models we aim to provide are predicated on the creation and implementation of these rules. Our experience so far points to the potential for overcoming technical barriers through persistence, flexibility, and cultivation of mutually beneficial collaborations.

5. Acknowledgements

This project is funded by NHPRC Records Projects grant NAR08-RE-10010-08, "Distributed Custodial Archival Preservation Environments", 2008-2011.

6. References

[1] J. Ward, T. Russell, A. Chassanoff, "Building a Trusted Distributed Archival Preservation with iRODS,", poster submission to the iRODS User meeting in Chapel Hill, March 24-26, 2010.

[2] iRODS: Data Grids, Digital Libraries, Persistent Archives, and Real-time Data Systems. http://www.irods.org

[3] Draft Recommendation for Space Data System Practices, CCSDS 652.0-R-1, "Audit and Certification of Trustworthy Digital Repositories"., October 2009.

Appendix

Initial ISO MOIMS-RAC Capabilities and Mapping to DCAPE Rules
RAC Numbers are from the "Combined Annotated document" Wiki page
http://wiki.digitalrepositoryauditandcertification.org/bin/view/Main/CombinedMetricsDocumentsFollowingFaceToFace
Accessed Sept. 2009

ISO Item	RAC No.	DCAPE Item	ISO Criteria	DCAPE Machine-Actionable Rule
1	A3.2.2 A5.1.3 A.5.1.4 A5.2		Address liability and challenges to ownership/rights.	Map from submission template to access and distribution controls
2	B1.1	DCAPE 4	Identify the content information and the information properties that the repository will preserve.	Define templates that specify required metadata and parameters for rules that are required to enforce properties
3	B1.1.2		Maintain a record of the Content Information and the Information Properties that it will preserve.	Link submission and policy templates to the preserved collection
4	B1.3	DCAPE 3	Specify Submission Information Package format (SIP)	Define templates that specify structure of a SIP and required content of a SIP.
5	B1.4	DCAPE 1	Verify the depositor of all materials.	Ingest data through a staging area that has a separate account for each depositor.
6	B1.5	DCAPE 6	Verify each SIP for completeness and correctness	Compare content of each SIP against template.
7	B1.6	DCAPE 8	Maintain the chain of custody during preservation.	Manage audit trails that document the identity of the archivist initiating the task
8	B1.7	DCAPE 22	Document the ingestion process and report to the producer	Send e-mail message to producer when process flags are set.
9	B1.8	DCAPE 10	Document administration processes that are relevant to content acquisition.	Maintain list of rules that govern management of the archives
10	B2.1 B2.1.1	DCAPE 13	Specify Archival Information Package format (AIP)	Define templates that specify structure of an AIP and required content of an AIP.
11	B2.1.2		Label the types of AIPs.	Store AIP type with each collection.

ISO Item	RAC No.	DCAPE Item	ISO Criteria	DCAPE Machine-Actionable Rule
12	B2.2	DCAPE 13	Specify how AIPs are constructed from SIPs.	Define transformation rule based on parsing of SIP template and AIP template
13	B2.3 B2.3.1	DCAPE 14	Document the final disposition of all SIPs	Maintain an audit trail for all SIPs
14	B2.4 B2.4.1 B2.4.1.1 B2.4.1.2 B2.4.1.3		Generate persistent, unique identifiers for all AIPs.	Define unique persistent logical name for each AIP
15	B2.4.1.4 B2.4.1.5		Verify uniqueness of identifiers.	Identifier uniqueness enforced by algorithm that assigns identifiers
16	B2.4.2		Manage mapping from unique identifier to physical storage location.	Storage location mapping enforced by iRODS data grid framework
17	B2.5	DCAPE 19	Provide authoritative representation information for all digital objects.	Define template specifying required representation information.
18	B2.5 B2.5.1	DCAPE 7	Identify the file type of all submitted Data Objects.	Apply type identification routine to each object on ingestion.
19	B2.6 B2.6.1		Document processes for acquiring preservation description information (PDI)	Define rule set that will be applied to extract PDI.
20	B2.6.2		Execute the documented processes for acquiring PDI.	Apply PDI rules specific to a collection.
21	B2.6.3 B2.7 B2.7.1 B2.7.2 B2.7.3		Ensure link between the PDI and relevant Content Information.	Set PDI extraction flag as part of PDI extraction rules.
22	B2.8	DCAPE 14	Verify completeness and correctness of each AIP.	Compare AIP against template for required content.
23	B2.9	DCAPE 17	Verify the integrity of the repository collections/content.	Periodically evaluate checksums and compare with original checksum value.
24	B2.10 B3.1 B3.2	DCAPE 21	Record actions and administration processes that are relevant to AIP creation.	Maintain an audit trail of processing steps applied during AIP creation.
25	B4.1		Specify storage of AIPs down to the bit level.	Identify form of container used to implement an AIP.
26	B4.1.1		Preserve the Content Information of AIPs.	Manage replicas of each AIP
27	B4.1.2		Actively monitor the integrity of AIPs.	Periodically evaluate checksums.
28	B4.2 B4.2.1	DCAPE 21	Record actions and administration processes that are relevant to AIP storage.	Maintain an audit trail of processing steps applied during AIP storage.
29	B4.2.2	DCAPE 18	Prove compliance of operations on AIPs to submission agreement.	Parse audit trails to show all operations comply with submission rule template
30	B5.1	DCAPE 24	Specify minimum descriptive information requirements to enable discovery.	Define submission template for required descriptive metadata.

ISO Item	RAC No.	DCAPE Item	ISO Criteria	DCAPE Machine-Actionable Rule
31	B5.2	DCAPE 11	Generate minimum descriptive metadata and associate with the AIP.	Apply rule to extract metadata specified within submission agreement.
32	B5.3 B5.3.1		Maintain link between each AIP and its descriptive information.	Package descriptive metadata within the AIP as an XML file
33	B6.1	DCAPE 9	Enforce access policies.	Authenticate all users, authorize all operations
34	B6.1.1	DCAPE 23	Log and review all access failures and anomalies.	Periodically parse audit trails and summarize access failures
35	B6.2	DCAPE 26	Disseminate authentic copies of records	Define template to specify creation of a Dissemination Information Package (DIP)
36	C1.1.2	DCAPE 15	Maintain replicas of all records, both content and representation information	Periodically snapshot metadata catalog, and maintain at least two replicas
37	C1.1.3	DCAPE 12	Detect bit corruption or loss.	Periodically validate checksums
38	C1.1.3.1	DCAPE 16	Report all incidents of data corruption or loss and repair/replace lost data	Periodically synchronize replicas, and generate and store report
39	C1.1.5	DCAPE 19	Manage migration to new hardware and media	Replicate AIPs to new storage system
40	C1.1.6		Document processes that enforce management policies	Maintain copy of the rule base and micro-services used for each collection
41	C1.1.6.1		Document changes to policies and processes	Version policies and micro-services
42	C1.1.6.1.1		Test and evaluate the effect of changes to the repository's critical processes.	Version state information attributes.
43	C1.2.1		Synchronize replicas	Periodically synchronize replicas
44	C2.3		Delineate roles, responsibilities, and authorization for archivist initiated changes	Define archivist roles and limit execution of preservation procedures to the archivist role
45	C2.4 B2.5.2		Maintain an off-site backup of all preserved information	Federate two independent iRODS data grids and replicate digital holdings
46	B2.5.3		Maintain access to the requisite Representation Information.	Manage Representation Information as metadata attributes on each record
47	B6.2.1 C1.1.1 C1.1.1.1 C1.1.1.2 C1.1.1.3 C1.1.1.4 C1.1.1.5 C1.1.1.6		Maintain and correct problem reports about errors in data or responses from users.	Parse audit trails for unsuccessful operations and design appropriate micro-service recovery mechanisms
48		DCAPE 24	Provide a search interface.	
49		DCAPE 5	Perform a virus check.	
50		DCAPE 2	Implement a loading dock.	
51		DCAPE 20	Migrate records to new formats.	
52		DCAPE 25	Create and certify Dissemination Information Packages.	

iRODS User Applications – Posters

Distributed Data Sharing with PetaShare for Collaborative Research

PetaShare Team, LSU

1. Introduction

The NSF-funded PetaShare project started in August 2006 with the goal of enabling transparent handling of underlying data sharing, archival, and retrieval mechanisms, and making data available to scientists across the state of Louisiana for analysis and visualization on demand. The goal has been to enable scientists to focus on their primary research problems, assured that the underlying infrastructure will manage the low-level data handling issues. The key technologies that are developed as a part of PetaShare include data-aware storage systems and data-aware schedulers, which take the responsibility of managing data resources and scheduling data tasks from the user and performing these tasks transparently. Petashare has two major components – an enhanced version of iRODS to provide a global name space and efficient data access among geographically distributed storage resources, and the Stork data placement scheduler which takes the responsibility of managing data resources and scheduling data tasks from the user and performing these tasks transparently.

PetaShare has been deployed across five state universities and two health sciences centers in Louisiana. These institutions include Louisiana State University (LSU), Tulane University, University of New Orleans, University of Louisiana at Lafayette, Louisiana Tech University, and LSU Health Sciences Centers in New Orleans and Shreveport. PetaShare manages approximately 300 Terabytes of disk storage distributed across these sites as well as 400 Terabytes of tape storage centrally located nearby LSU campus. For connecting all of the participating sites together, PetaShare leverages LONI, which is a statewide 40 Gbps fiber-optic network in Louisiana. It links all major research institutes in Louisiana.

2. iRODS in PetaShare

iRODS has been the backbone of Petashare, providing a global name space across all participating institutions. Since its initial implementation, PetaShare has gone through major changes such as integration of MASREP (A Multi-master ASynchronous REPlication) tool, which asynchronously replicates metadata to all other sites to eliminate single point of failure and to provide high

availability without sacrificing performance. MASREP even increases the performance because all incoming metadata requests from a respective server are processed within that site. At the front-end, PetaShare provides very light weight interfaces called PetaFs, Petashell, and Pcommands, based on FUSE, Parrot, and icommands technologies respectively. PetaFs is based on FUSE, and the client has recently been ported to Mac OSX which uses MacFUSE. The novel PetaFs and Petashell interfaces enable users to access their remote and distributed data the same way as they access the data on their local disk. While doing so, users need not make any changes to their application, including re-compiling or re-linking, and they also do not need any special privileges on the system to use these interfaces.

PetaShare provides scientists with simple uniform interfaces to store, access, and process heterogeneous distributed data sources. The archived data is well cataloged to enable easy access to the desired files or segments of files, which can then be returned to the requester in a chosen format or resolution. Multiple copies of high priority information can be stored at different physical locations to increase reliability and also enable easier retrieval by scientists in different geographical locations. The data is also indexed to enable easy and efficient access to desired data. The requested data is moved from the source or archival sites to the computation sites for processing as required, and the results are then sent back to the interested parties for further analysis or back to the long-term storage sites for archival.

As of July 2009, PetaShare has been actively used for 25 different research projects by more than 70 senior researchers from 11 different institutions. The supported application areas include: coastal hazard prediction (LSU and SURA), reservoir uncertainty analysis (LSU, ULL, and SUBR), DNA sequencing (Tulane and UNO), high energy physics (LSU, Latech, and DOSAR), X-ray tomography (LSU), numerical relativity (LSU), high speed visualization (LSU and ULL), biomedical data mining (LSUHSC, LSU and Latech), and computational fluid dynamics (LSU). PetaShare has also been an important component in several other state-wide cyberinfrastructure projects in Louisiana such as the NSF-funded CyberTools and HPCOPS, the

iRODS User Group Meeting 2010

39

Louisiana BoR funded LONI Institute, and the DOE-funded UCoMS projects.

A Note on PetaFs

A virtual filesystem that allows users to access PetaShare resources as a local filesystem after being mounted on their machines. By using PetaFs, PetaShare resources can be seen in the directory hierarchy of an existing filesystem and accessed in the same way as local storage. PetaFs is based on FUSE (Filesystem in Userspace), a simple interface to export a virtual filesystem to the Linux kernel in userspace. PetaFs translates local I/O calls into remote iRODS calls through intermediate FUSE library calls. In the kernel, FUSE incorporates with the real filesystem and maps these FUSE calls to the actual filesystem calls at one end, and to the remote iRODS calls at the other end. Communication between kernel module and FUSE library is established by specifying a file descriptor obtained from /dev/fuse device file. This file descriptor is passed to the mount system call to match up the file descriptor with the mounted PetaFs virtual filesystem. The advantage of PetaFs is that it makes it possible to work on the data stored in Petashare resources by using standard UNIX commands (ls, cp, etc) and system calls (open, read, write, etc.) as in the real filesystem.

UNC Information Technology Services

William Schulz

UNC Information Technology Services (ITS)

The Research Computing unit at UNC Chapel Hill, a division of Information Technology Services (ITS), has been hosting several production iRODS servers for more than one year. These instances provide different sets of functionality and storage capabilities to a variety of groups both at UNC and collaborating institutions.

The Research Computing group in ITS is uniquely positioned to assist a large existing user base among many departments at UNC, as it provides the University with most of its HPC infrastructure. In addition to the computational capability provided by several large clusters, Research Computing hosts high performance storage and archiving systems.

A request to provide tape storage for an iRODS grid hosted by the Renaissance Computing Institute (RENCI) led to the first RECO iRODS server. This instance became part of the DICE Center's NARA prototype grid at RENCI, and continues to provide several collections with tape storage.

UNC's Institute for the Environment, long a user of RECO's services, looked to iRODS as a way of managing, storing, and distributing a large collection of federally generated data. This collection is made freely available to researchers worldwide through a browser front end. Leveraging the iRODS Java API, a web application allows users to search the collection's rich set of object-level metadata.

The Carolina Digital Repository, developed by the UNC University Library, is an institutional digital repository that leverages iRODS for its data store. ITS Research Computing is providing iRODS configuration assistance and hosts the iRODS server responsible for archival storage.

This presentation will provide an overview of how the Research Computing iRODS servers are configured differently for their varied collections, with an explanation of basic simple policy and maintenance rules.

The ARCS Data Fabric

Shunde Zhang (shunde.zhang@arcs.org.au), Florian Goessmann, Pauline Mak

The Australian Research Collaboration Service (ARCS)

Overview

The Australian Research Collaboration Service (ARCS) Data Fabric was developed as a solution for the growing need by researchers to easily store their research data, and to share that data across institutional boundaries. As such, it is a generic service that is not tied to any specific kinds of data or research disciplines and is available to every Australian researcher and their international collaborators.

Access to the ARCS webDrive is possible through either a WebDAV client such as Windows Explorer and Mac OS Finder, and any modern web browser. Dedicated areas of the ARCS webDrive can be accessed using the OPeNDAP protocol through the ARCS OPeNDAP Network and Digital Library. The authentication mechanism of the ARCS webDrive has been designed to be use methods and technologies supported by the Australian Access Federation (AAF).

1. Architecture

The ARCS Data Fabric consists of two modules: the ARCS webDrive and the ARCS OPeNDAP Network and Digital Library. They are both based on iRODS, the Integrated Rule-Oriented Data System, where data is stored.

1.1. ARCS webDrive

The ARCS webDrive as two distinct layers, a back-end and a front-end. The back-end interfaces with the physical storage, whereas the front-end provides the different interfaces to the user.

The back-end of the ARCS webDrive is iRODS, which sits on top of physical, large-scale storage infrastructure hosted by and provided through the Members of ARCS (MARCS). This setup allows the ARCS webDrive to be expandable and fault tolerant, as it does not have to rely solely on one physical storage system.

The front-end, Davis, of the ARCS webDrive is a development by ARCS Data Services. It provides two easy-to-use interfaces: a WebDAV server and web browser access. The WebDAV server allows researchers to access and store data in the ARCS webDrive with any WebDAV client including those built into operating systems such as Windows XP and Mac OS X. The web access is available through most modern web browsers. In addition to

uploading and downloading data, the web interface also offers access control mechanisms, metadata for files and collections, as well as the 'trash can'.

1.2. Data Sharing and Access Control

Giving researchers the ability to share data was the main drive for the development of the ARCS webDrive. As a result, the ARCS webDrive puts sophisticated access control mechanisms at the disposal of the researcher. It is possible to assign access of different levels (read, write, own) to single files or whole collections and to individuals or groups.

If a group of researchers frequently shares files, they can request for a group to be created for them. This further simplifies sharing of data as each group owns a group collection, which makes all data stored in it immediately available to all group members.

1.3. ARCS OPeNDAP Network and Digital Library

The system consists of two distinct parts: a network of data servers, and a portal which harvests and catalogues information on all datasets handled by all data servers in the network.

The data servers run THREDDS Data Server (TDS), an implementation of the DAP protocol. This protocol was designed for the delivery of scientific data over the web and is well established in the ocean, climate, and remote sensing sciences communities. At this stage, ARCS hosts five TDS servers, based at Members of ARCS (MARCS), closest to the Integrated Marine Observing System (IMOS) facilities.

The TDS servers are co-located with the servers for the ARCS webDrive and have access the underlying storage system. This setup makes data stored in the ARCS webDrive available through the ARCS OPeNDAP Network.

The digital library component is provided by an instance of the Tasmanian Partnership for Advanced Computing (TPAC) Digital Library. The digital library provides a single front-end to all datasets available through any of the data servers, and hence enables researchers to discover datasets without prior knowledge of their physical location.

2. Current setup

Currently, seven iRODS nodes have been set up in each capital city of Australia. They are all in one iRODS zone, with one being the master zone and iRODS Metadata Catalog (iCAT), and others being slaves. Most sites have hierarchical storage, such as tape device, in the back-end. To date there are more than 18 TB of data stored and 280 users registered in the Data Fabric. Users and storage have nearly tripled in the last year.

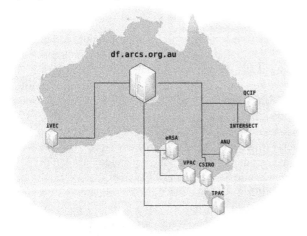

3. Use Cases

While the ARCS Data Fabric is being used every day by individuals to store and share data, it is also integrated with eResearch service providers external to ARCS. For example, the Australian Synchrotron's Virtual Beam Line data portal was developed to give users of the synchrotron an easy way to transport the results of experiments off the facilities to storage that provides access to data from their home institution. ARCS Data Services and the developers at the synchrotron have successfully worked together to integrate the ARCS Data Fabric as a storage selectable target for the data transport mechanism.

Another function has also been developed and will be deployed soon to enable Data Fabric users to create Persistent IDs for Data Fabric objects in the persistent Identifier Service (PIDS) of the Australian National Data Service (ANDS). This is achieved by invoking predefined rules from the Davis web interface.

Building a Trusted Distributed Archival Preservation Service with iRODS

Jewel H. Ward, Terrell G. Russell, and Alexandra Chassanoff

School of Information and Library Science, University of North Carolina at Chapel Hill

Abstract

The Distributed Custodial Archival Preservation Environments (DCAPE) [1] project is a proof-of-concept of the viability of a distributed custodial preservation approach as a production service using iRODS [2]. The DCAPE partnership is comprised of 32 people across 10 institutions, as well as doctoral and graduate students. These partners include technologists, librarians, and archivists from computer science research, state libraries, and state, university, and cultural archives. In the first phase of this project, the project team created an initial set of 26 iRODS rules for use by the DCAPE archivists and administrators. We based these rules on the stated needs of the partner organizations and the standards developed to determine trustworthiness by the ISO Mission Operations Information Management System repository assessment criteria (ISO MOIMS-RAC) group [3,4]. Within the DCAPE project, the iRODS infrastructure serves two critical functions: (1) it validates the trustworthiness of the repository through the enactment of ISO-MOIMS-compliant policies; and, (2) it enables the distributed auditable administration of the repository through the invocation of iRODS rules.

Index Keyword Terms—Distributed Systems, Document/file management, Data Sharing, Online Information Services

1. Introduction

iRODS is extensible; rules may be added or deleted as needed by archivists and administrators. These rules are machine-actionable policies; that is, a repository administrator may enforce written policies at the machine level by re-writing the policies as code that can be read by the iRODS rule engine. These policies may also be enforced across a distributed environment, which provides a method for archivists in disparate locations to manage their records. The rule engine is dynamic; the rules may be installed or removed as the needs of the repository administrators change.

In the first phase of the 2-½ year DCAPE project, the team developed an initial set of 26 capabilities, based on the standards developed by the ISO MOIMS-RAC group. These capabilities include rules that manage Open Archival Information Systems (OAIS) compatible SIPs, AIPs, DIPs, identifiers, audit and security information, and enforce policies and service level agreements (SLAs), among others. The goal is to converge towards a set of fundamental building blocks necessary to create a distributed, trustworthy archival production system.

Preservation-as-a-Service (PaaS) is a potential business model that may prove viable as the technologies involved have become commodities and the availability of significant amounts of storage is common. Alongside bandwidth costs, the overhead associated with the management of preservation policy has become a limiting factor when dealing with large datasets. DCAPE aims to reduce this overhead and provide an archivist-level interface into a very powerful system.

In this poster, we describe the rationale for creating the DCAPE project, what we have accomplished so far, what we have learned, and what our future work on the project will entail.

2. Acknowledgements

This work is funded by the NHPRC Records Projects grant NHPRC RE10010-08, "Distributed Custodial Archival Preservation Environments" (2008-2011). We would like to think Richard Marciano for his comments on this poster.

3. References

[1] DCAPE project (Distributed Custodial Archival Preservation Environments), http://dcape.org.
[2] DICE, "Overview: Data Management & iRODS", iRODS Publications, San Diego, CA, March 19-20, 2009.
[3] MOIMS-RAC: Repository Audit and Certification working group, http://wiki.digitalrepositoryauditandcertification.org.
[4] M. Day. "Toward Distributed Infrastructures for Digital Preservation: The Roles of Collaboration and Trust", Journal of Digital Information, 1(3), College Station, TX, 2008.

2. Clients for iRODS

A Service-Oriented Interface to the iRODS Data Grid

Nicola Venuti[*], *Francesco Locunto*[*], *Michael Conway*[**], *Leesa Brieger*[◊]

[*]Nice S.r.l., [**]Data Intensive Cyber Environments Center, UNC, [◊]RENCI, UNC

Abstract

iRODS microservices and rules can be used to build a data grid that implements a community's own data policy. However, often the data administrators are not the developers who customize the services or deploy the data grid. A tool that gives the data administrator intuitive access to the rules and special-purpose services of their data grid is important in separating the IT tasks from the data administration tasks.

The EnginFrame (EF) cloud interface framework from Nice S.r.l. was used to build a service-oriented iRODS interface. This interface demonstrates how data grid access can be customized for community use; one view of the data grid, determined by data usage scenarios, is provided for the community user, and another view, determined by data management criteria, is provided for the administrative user.

Index Keyword Terms—iRODS data grid, data grid interface, data grid access, web interface, EnginFrame, EF, Grid Portal, cloud interface, administrative interface.

1. Introduction

Development of special-purpose microservices and rules will equip an iRODS data grid to implement specialized data access and preservation policy as required by a target community. The developers who would customize a data grid in this way may not, however, be the data administrators who determine and/or enforce data policy for that community.

Therefore, along with a customized data grid, it is imperative to offer a user-friendly interface that provides not only user access to community data, but also administrative access to the services that support and implement data policy. The data grid, with special-purpose services and with an administrative interface, then provides the data administrator with the necessary tools to curate and preserve his community's electronic data - without being an iRODS programmer to do it.

The user-friendly interface provides a separation between the data administrator and the systems administrator. It can offer intuitive access to the specialized data services, freeing up the data admin to concentrate on applying, enforcing, and verifying data policy for his community.

The authors used the EnginFrame (EF) cloud interface framework to develop a prototype of such an interface; this was used for a live demonstration of iRODS services at an NSF/NARA/NITRD iRODS presentation in August 2009. The interface was used to showcase important iRODS archival services in a real-time demo. It serves to illustrate how an interface can be customized to offer specialized views of the services implemented in a given data grid. Further, the interface presents one view of data and services for community users and another view, which includes more administrative functionalities, for the data administrator.

Several basic iRODS services were selected for the demonstration; we briefly mention implementation considerations for some of these special services, followed by a description of the EnginFrame interface and then the blending of the two technologies.

2. Specialized iRODS Services

While iRODS can be viewed as a framework for implementing data policy for the curation of electronic assets, it is also a tool kit that comes with many pre-defined rules, microservices, and capabilities. Some of these enable functionalities such as audit tracking and quota checking, in support of verification of policy; others enable capabilities such as searching on user-defined metadata.

These were the sorts of functionalities, based on out-of-the-box iRODS services, that were showcased at the NSF demo; thus these were the services exposed in the EF interface to the data grid.

2.1. Audit Tracking

Audit tracking is enabled in iRODS by changing the setting of the parameter auditEnabled from "0" to "2" in iRODS_root/server/icat/src/icatMidLevelRoutines.c, then recompiling, and restarting the iRODS server. Once audit tracking is enabled, any operation that calls upon the iCAT metadata catalogue is logged - in the iCAT. Any requests, such as downloading a data object, changing permissions on a collection, deleting or creating an object, etc., are all logged in the iCAT's audit table, along with record of the change that was made if authorization for the operation was granted. Audit information can then be tracked by querying this table and presenting the results in a user-friendly format. The queries can be implemented with the *iquest* icommand or with microservices by using msiMakeGenQuery and msiExecGenQuery.

There is a need to be careful, however, with these queries. The microservice queries use an iRODS-specific syntax to approximate SQL but does not repli–cate it perfectly. Iquest allows a reduced form of SQL querying. Neither approach yet gives full SQL functionality. For audit table querying, there is a further complication that can result in spurious results. Consider that the audit table in the iCAT database contains the following fields:

    AUDIT_OBJ_ID
    AUDIT_USER_ID
    AUDIT_ACTION_ID
    AUDIT_COMMENT
    AUDIT_CREATE_TIME
    AUDIT_MODIFY_TIME

The audit table, in AUDIT_OBJ_ID, contains information about the entity (data object, collection, resource, user, etc.,) that is the object of an action that was performed and logged. It contains the ID of the target entity; however, there is no built-in mechanism to determine which it is - object, collection, user, resource, etc. Thus, at any one time, the AUDIT_OBJ_ID field of the audit table can refer to any of a number of tables containing detailed information on either a data object, a collection, a user, or a resource. The joins of the standard iRODS query services then have the effect of joining all the tables referred to by the ID, with the result that much spurious information is retrieved with the query.

By breaking down the joins into a series of simpler *iquest* queries, it is possible to separately query on each type of entity in the audit table, thereby avoiding the joins that cause spurious results to be generated. The following example for an audit procedure for an administrative user illustrates this; the *iquest* commands are run in a script so that output can be saved from one step to the next.

1.To see an audit trail for a given user, save an iRODS user name into a script variable and run the iquest *command to query the audit table:*

    iquest "SELECT AUDIT_OBJ_ID,
        AUDIT_ACTION_ID, AUDIT_COMMENT,
        AUDIT_CREATE_TIME,
        AUDIT_MODIFY_TIME WHERE
        USER_NAME = '${_irods_username}'

2. Save the AUDIT_OBJ_ID into a script variable and use it to get query and get separate results from each entity table:

    iquest "SELECT COLL_NAME, DATA_NAME
        WHERE DATA_ID = '${_objId}'"

    iquest "SELECT COLL_NAME WHERE
        COLL_ID = '${_objId}'"

    iquest "SELECT USER_NAME WHERE
        USER_ID = '${_objId}'"

For the NSF/NARA demo, the results of these queries were arranged into xml files to allow for formatted presentation. Additional Java filters provide an easy way to further manipulate the results and were applied in order to sort and refine the search results.

2.2. Other Services

iRODS allows users to add their own AVU triplets (attribute, value, units) to the iCAT metadata catalogue. Metadata searching of user-defined metadata was implemented for the demo using the *iquest* icommand to query the iCAT.

The implementation of quotas is awaited in iRODS and should be coming out in version 2.3. In the meantime, it is possible to use *iquest* to return and display usage information for each user, handling it similarly to the way quota information will be handled. This was implemented in the demo prototype.

The *irule* icommand allows users to run any iRODS rules on a command line. The interface also provided a means of pointing and clicking to edit and run selected rules.

3. EnginFrame

EnginFrame is proprietary software developed by Nice S.r.l. It is typically used as a computational grid portal or a cloud interface and serves as a framework for logically collecting applications, services and resources and presenting them in a web 2.0 interface that provides user-friendly access to the distributed resources. It is not a portlet container but instead delivers services that are JSR168-compliant; EnginFrame allows organizations to provide application-oriented computing and data services to both users (via Web browsers) and in-house or ISV applications (via SOAP/WSDL based Web services) so EF services could be used as portlets in another portal.

The main goal of EF is to hide the details and the complexity of the underlying infrastructure in order to improve usability and utilization. Usability goes up when end-user requirements for accessing the

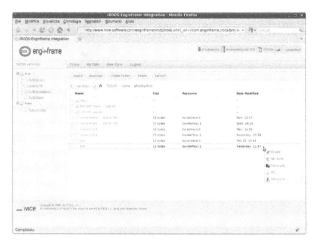

Figure 1. Metadata and ACL settings can be viewed and modified through the browser.

infrastructure go down, and utilization is improved by making the evolution of the underlying systems trans– parent to the end-user and enforcing the utilization policies even as infrastructure evolves.

EF provides a flexible authentication framework with built-in support for a wide set of well-known authentication mechanisms like OS/NIS/PAM, LDAP, and Microsoft Active Directory. It has been integrated with the iRODS challenge-response authentication mechanism. The EF authorization framework allows the definition of groups of users and access control lists, thus providing a means for tailoring the Web interface to the specific users' roles or access rights. This was used in the demo interface to distinguish between community users and administrative users of the data grid. Community users were presented, in the interface, a reduced set of services compared to administrative users.

4. The iRODS EF Interface

The merging of the EnginFrame and iRODS technologies required development of an iRODS plug-in for EF and the wrapping of the iRODS services as EF services. The EF file manager for data browsing was also outfitted with iRODS functionalities so that some of the basic iRODS characteristics are present in the data browser.

User-defined metadata can be added, modified, queried, and deleted as part of basic iRODS functionalities. Setting and modifying ACL permissions are also included among the basic iRODS capabilities. Both these functionalities are available with the browser through the EF interface. See Figure 1.

Disk usage is queried using *iquest* and displayed.

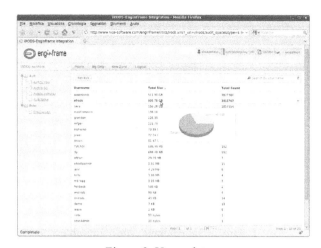

Figure 2. Usage data

The same sort of display is planned for quotas when that functionality becomes operational. See Figure 2.

Figure 3 shows the unfiltered results of an audit table query on all entries, and Figure 4 is a snapshot of the rule editor.

5. Deploying Data Grids

The customization of a data grid for a user community is an important step in deploying this technology for a given user group. Beyond simply installing the data grid, data management policy must be unambiguously defined and then translated into the microservices and rules of this technology.

Another very important step in the deployment is the development of a user-friendly interface for accessing the data grid. A custom interface can provide intuitive access to the custom services of the data grid and a user-friendly way of invoking the rules that implement and enforce data policy.

Further, the interface can be customized to various user groups that access the data and data services. As mentioned above, the EF interface was developed to show different views of the services to community and administrative users, thereby distinguishing between the different classes of services offered to the two groups. It would also be possible to adjust the view of the data grid to other user groups, so that the presentation of data and services fits with a group's own use cases.

6. The Future

A new domain of expertise will likely grow up around this technology, embodied in those who deploy iRODS data grids. They will likely become increasingly separate from the DICE developers of iRODS as well as user communities who make use of iRODS technology. There is a need for a third group that bridges the gap between these two. The developers know all that this

Figure 3. Data dump of the audit table

Figure 4. The rule editor

technology can offer, but are often not aware of the intricate details of the needs of the user groups. Users know some rudimentary aspects of the data grids but often define their needs in terms of the constraints they have learned to live with rather than exploiting the full potential of iRODS. There is increasingly a need for a group that straddles those two perspectives and brings rich iRODS capabilities to user groups with complex data needs.

These deployment groups must work closely with data specialists from the user communities in order to understand the required policy to implement in the data grids and how the administrative interfaces should operate. They will also have to understand how the users must view the data and services presented in order to meet their use cases. Policy should become easy to apply using the custom interface, and the full functionality of rich iRODS services should be delivered.

Deployment groups will promote the adoption of iRODS data grids, supporting communities who want to explore the technology, and allowing its adoption even by groups who may not be well-supported with in-house IT specialists. The deployment groups will do the programming of the services and the development of the interfaces so that users and data administrators will be freed from these tasks. The upshot is that many more communities will have access to this technology.

7. References

[1] Reagan W. Moore, Richard Marciano, Arcot Rajasekar, Antoine de Torcy, Chien-Yi Hou, Leesa Brieger, Jon Crabtree, Jewel Ward, Mason Chua, UNC Chapel Hill; Wayne Schroeder, Michael Wan, Sheau-Yen Chen, UCSD, "NITRD iRODS Demonstration", sponsored by NARA at NSF, 2009. *Can be linked from https://www.irods.org/index.php/Publications.* "Technical Demonstration of Integrated Preservation Infrastructure Prototype", National Coordination Office for Information Technology Research and Development (NITRD) / NSF / NARA, National Science Foundation, Washington, D.C., August 4, 2009 Powerpoint Version. Combined Video and Powerpoint Slides of NITRD Demo. *Can be linked from https://www.irods.org/index.php/Publications.*
[2] iRODS and Data Preservation 2nd Workshop on Data Preservation and Long Term Analysis in HEP, Wayne Schroeder, SLAC National Accelerator Laboratory, Menlo Park, CA, May 26, 2009. *Can be linked from https://www.irods.org/index.php/Publications.*
[3] Policy-Based Distributed Data Management Systems, Open Repositories 09, Reagan Moore, Arcot Rajasekar, Mike Wan, May, 2009. *Can be linked from https://www.irods.org/index.php/Publications.*
[4] http://www.nice-software.com
[5] http://www.enginframe.com
[6] http://code.google.com/p/ef-irods-plugin/

iExplore for iRODS Distributed Data Management

Bing Zhu

Data Intensive Cyber Environments Group, Institute for Neural Computation
University of California, San Diego, bizhu@ucsd.edu

Abstract

iExplore is a graphical user interface client tool for navigation and manipulation of data within the iRODS distributed data system. Designed and implemented in the Windows platform, it offers a rich set of functions with excellent performance for iRODS users.

Index Keyword Terms—Graphical User Interface, iRODS Client Tool, Data Manipulation, Windows Platform.

1. Introduction

iExplorer is a graphic user interface tool that runs on the Windows platform for browsing distributed data and related digital information managed by iRODS, the Integrated Rule-Oriented Data System [1, 2]. iExplore supports a rich set of iRODS client functions through its main browser window, which comprises a tree display and a list box showing the hierarchical collection structure and the content of the selected collection that is stored in a distributed iRODS environment, federated data grid, or heterogeneous storage systems, etc.

iExplore is developed using the Microsoft Foundation Class (MFC) with enabled .net GUI features. iExplore interacts with iRODS through the iRODS client library, which issues the iRODS communication protocol [3], an RPC-based client-server software package developed by iRODS team. Fig. 1 shows a snapshot of the main screen.

iExplore software can be downloaded from the iRODS web site at: https://www.irods.org/index.php/windows. Since it is developed using the original iRODS C library and Microsoft C++ within the user interface, iExplore demonstrates superb performance for all data manipulation operations.

2. Functions and Dialogs

iExplore provides many client functions through its GUI implementation, such as iRODS file system browsing, file/collection downloading, file/collection uploading, searching, and metadata editing. Below are detailed descriptions of the functions and dialogs implemented in the current version of iExplore. Some new features introduced in the latest release will be described in a separate section.

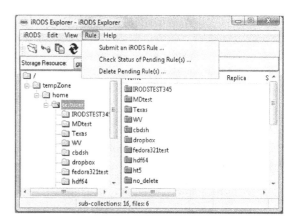

Fig 1. The main screen of iExplore

1. **Navigation of hierarchical structure**: Navigation within an iRODS collection and datasets is through either a tree view or a list in the main screen.
2. **Uploading files/folders**: Users can use the menu to launch a file or folder selection dialog to upload files or folders into iRODS. The storage resource is determined by the resource combo box above the tree.
3. **Downloading datasets**: iRODS files can be downloaded to a local disk through the download menu. Users will be asked to select a local folder for downloading files.
4. **Data Replication**: Users can make replicas of selected files or a collection through "Replicate" menu.
5. **Data Access Control**: A user can set data access permissions on files for other users.
6. **Manipulation of metadata**: A metadata dialog allows users to enter, edit, and view metadata.
7. **Change Password**: The change password dialog allows a user to change their password.
8. **iRODS Rules**: The "Rule" menu supports three submenus for submitting rules, checking rule status, and deleting a submitted rule.
9. **Online help**: iExplore has a link in its About dialog that directs users to iRODS on-line documents for full descriptions of the iRODS system and various operations.

3. New Features in Latest Release

The following new features were introduced in the latest release of iExplore.

1. **Job Progress Indicator**: A job progress indicator has been implemented to show the progress of tasks in uploading and downloading files or collections. Usually the GUI progress indicator is hidden in the main window next to the resource selection field. It will automatically appear when a job starts.

2. **HTML information display**: An HTML display was introduced in the latest release to display information about distributed stores, user, and metadata in tabular form, a more user-friendly representation of the information.

3. **Search Dialog**: A new search dialog allows user to search on patterns in file and user-defined metadata. Although the search criteria is like a database query language, a simple query such as the "contain" operation is quite intuitive, and users will find this search very useful.

4. Proposed Future Development

As Microsoft technologies evolve, and based on user requests, iExplore will continue to evolve to provide additional iRODS functions and interfaces for new technologies.

1. **New main screen**: This has an extra pane to show rich information: thumbnail, system metadata, user metadata, as shown in Fig 2.

Fig 2. A Proposed iExplore Main Screen. A third pane will be added in the right panel to display thumbnails, metadata, properties, etc.

2. **Multi-Language Support**: New development will provide multi-language support through Microsoft UNICODE implementation.

3. **Generic Interface** for integration with other software applications: New development of iExplore will look into incorporation of the Windows Presentation Foundation so that it can be easily integrated with other applications, map applications, data cube displays, multi-media software, numerous web applications, etc.

4. **A generic interface** for iRODS Plug-play modules such as automatic metadata extraction, thumbnail creation, etc.

5. **New Rule Editor**: A new user-friendly iRODS rule editor will allow users to navigate through the list of available iRODS micro-services in a server to construct new iRODS rules. There will be a check that verifies iRODS rule syntax.

6. **Advanced Search**: The Advanced Search will allow experienced users to conduct more complex searches against iRODS distributed stores. The advanced search will also keep track of user search patterns and provide intelligent assistance for users.

5. Summary

iExplore is an efficient client tool for navigating the iRODS distributed data system. It offers a rich set of functions and user dialogs that are convenient and easy to use for iRODS users. Future development will include rich data representations such as auto-display of thumbnail images, movie proxies, and metadata by combining the latest Microsoft technologies such as Windows Presentation Foundation.

7. References

[1] iRODS: Data Grids, Digital Libraries, Persistent Archives, and Real-time Data Systems. www.irods.org.

[2] R. Moore, A. Rajasekar, M. Wan, and W Schroeder. Policy-Based Distributed Data Management Systems. The 4th International Conference on Open Repositories. Atlanta, Georgia. May 19, 2009.

[3] Michael Wan, Reagan Moore, Arcot Rajasekar. Distributed Shared Collection Communication Protocol. https://www.irods.org/pubs/DICE_irodsProtPaper.pdf.

[4] Introduction to Windows Presentation Foundation. http://msdn.microsoft.com/en-us/library/aa970268.aspx.

The Development of Digital Archives Management Tools for iRODS

Tsung-Tai Yeh[a], Hsin-Wen Wei[a], Shin-Hao Liu[a], Pei-Chi Huang[b], Tsan-sheng Hsu[a], Yen-Chiu Chen[b]

[a] *Institute of Information Science, Academia Sinica Taipei, Taiwan*
[b] *Department of Computer Science, Tsing Hua University, Taiwan*
E-mail: {b8875,hwwei, kofman, peggy1105, tshsu, yenchiu}@iis.sinica.edu.tw

Abstract

The amount of digital data in today's society is both enormous and constantly growing. Unfortunately, existing digital archives are often fragile and susceptible to data loss. Thus, as the amount of digital information continues to grow almost exponentially, it is increasingly important to develop new ways to manipulate this data and minimize the risk of data loss after hardware failures. In this paper, we create an improved data preservation system by working with iRODS, a distributed data management system suitable for data grids, digital libraries, and persistent archives. We develop a user interface, called UrSpace, provide a corresponding Sync Package, and also create a monitoring system (call SIMS) that can check iRODS for errors and monitor the system independently. These tools and system are currently used for the TELDAP program in Taiwan.

Index Keyword Terms—TELDAP, Data Preservation.

1. Introduction

In the digital age, all forms of data such as text, pictures, music and video are available in digital format, and thus the need for storage capacity is constantly growing. When organizations such as the IDC (International Data Corporation) report that the digital universe doubles every 18 months [2], it is certain that data users will face unimaginably large amounts of data in the near future. In order to keep pace with this immense increase in information, it is necessary to create an extensive but manageable data preservation framework that enables people to agilely handle colossal amounts of data.[3]

One of the greatest challenges with existing data management is that these archives are fragile, and they are often prone to crash in unexpected ways. Generally, digital archives are stored in some type of electronic storage device, but due to inevitable malfunctions and wear, no existing digital archives can remain operational forever. As a result, there is a continuous need to develop increasingly reliable preservation mechanisms in order to ensure that data is consistently accessible and robust.

In 2002, a "National Digital Archive Project" (NDAP) was initiated and worked to collect and integrate different kinds of digital archives from institutes, museums and research groups from across Taiwan. Created in 2008, the "Taiwan e-Learning and Digital Archives Program" (TELDAP) [3] continues the work of NDAP. In order to reliably manage all of this data, the Digital Archives Remote-Backup (DARB) project was proposed. Its primary responsibilities include data preservation system development and research. The DARB project also created the Sinica Data Preservation System (SIDPS), which stores digital archives and content from such diverse field as history, biology, ethnology, education and language.

SIDPS follows a distributed framework and manipulates data in multi-level collections. The characteristics of this design are to meet the performance of data preservation in the distributed environment and alleviate the cost of external network deployment. In maintaining SIDPS, DARB works closely with another data management system, specifically designed for working with data grids, called the Integrated Rule-Oriented Data System (iRODS) [4]. Taking advantage of rule-based policy mechanisms, iRODS provides several optimized data transfer functions, and it enables users to more flexibly coordinate data stored within distributed environments. This feature allows the DARB project to use iRODS to manage digital archives stored in different institutes across Taiwan.

Generally, the iRODS team provides several APIs for developers to create their applications. It is true that there are some iRODS user interfaces such as Davis WebDAV [9] and iRODS Explorer for Windows. However, users who aim to preserve digital data need a good interface that is multilingual, a convenient process to make data preservation easier and safer, and a fast data transfer mechanism. Hence, the DARB team takes advantage of iRODS' APIs to develop a user interface called the UrSpace tool, and a corresponding data preservation utility, called the Sync Package. The system status of iRODS is tracked through the Sinica iRODS monitoring System (SIMS), which detects errors that occur within the iRODS system and quickly alerts system administrators of any problems.

---

[3] Supported in part by National Science Council (Taiwan) Grants NSC99-2631-H-001-024.

The remainder of this paper is organized as follows. We first describe the SIDPS framework, and then outline the designs of the UrSpace interface and the Sync Package utility. Next we introduce SIMS, the monitoring system for iRODS. Lastly, in the final section we present our conclusions.

2. Digital Archives Preservation Cyberinfrastrature

Recently, the number of digital archives stored within SIDPS has grown rapidly. In order to handle this increased data flow, we propose a digital archives support framework that is based on the iRODS system and designed to coordinate the aggregation and preservation of archival data. Its key roles include handling distributed data acquisition, data storage, integration, transformation, and management.

2.1 The Multi-level Digital Archive Collection

The architecture for a multi-level digital archive collection like SIDPS requires a fast data transfer speed, low power consumption, and a disaster recovery mechanism. In regards to data transfer rates, we employ a framework designed to overcome issues related to limited network bandwidth while also improving the cost-effectiveness of data preservation. As Figure 1 demonstrates, this framework can be broadly divided into three levels.

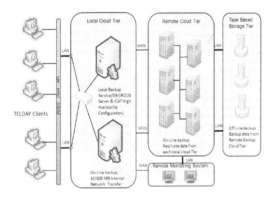

Figure 1 Multi-level Digital Archive Collection

First, the local cloud tier provides a storage buffer. Users are able to upload digital archives to their local storage devices at high speed. Second, the SIDPS located within the remote cloud tier moves digital archives that have not been modified or have been left idle over a period of time to the SIDPS. Lastly, tape servers regularly replicate digital archives from the SIDPS. Overall this multi-level digital archive collection framework shortens data uploading time, because users only need to upload their data through their internal network, rather than through the much slower external network. This framework

also helps reduce power consumption, because backup copies of the data are stored within the internal network on tape, compared to more power-intensive online models such as Hadoop [8] or the google file system [7]. Most of the time, the tape storage system is kept off-line, and is only used during periodic backup sessions or when original data needs to be recovered due to errors within the SIDPS. Throughout this process, the SIMS monitoring system acts as a gatekeeper, serving to monitor each data transaction at each of the different institutes, and to then immediately notify system administrators of errors via e-mail or instant message.

3. The UrSpace Tool

A good user interface ought to match system operations to the real world. Generally speaking, users that join TELDAP program would like to have a good user tool that supports multilingual interface, provides a view of the system status, and provides flexible and efficient functionalities. UrSpace is a Graphical User Interface (GUI) tool based on the iRODS Jargon APIs. The objective of the UrSpace tool is to provide users with a friendly and multilingual interface to manage metadata and upload and download digital archives to and from the iRODS system. The tool itself is compatible with multiple operating systems (unlike the iRODS Explorer for Windows), and performs the following functions: multiple data transfers, resume transfers, export log files to PDF format, edit metadata, and basic searches. UrSpace is also free and can be downloaded from the DARB website [5]. The Davis WebDAV interface [9] is also based on Jargon APIs and includes several convenient functions that help users manipulate data easily. The UrSpace tool is focused on developing useful data manipulation mechanisms and efficient data transfer methods in a multilingual interface. Overall, the UrSpace tool offers users who are not familiar with command-line operations a more approachable alternative.

3.1 UrSpace Features

The UrSpace tool is a multi-function user interface. It is mainly composed of several Java packages and Jargon APIs. The Java Jargon APIs released by the iRODS team contain several data manipulation functions such as file I/O access, GSI authentication modules and metadata operations. This interface itself was designed using the Java Swing Library. As Figure 2 shows, the DARB team uses the Jargon APIs to complete basic data manipulation tasks, such as data uploading, downloading, metadata editing, and MD5 check sum verification. The Java multi-thread library is also used to design the "multiple tasks" processing function, and the Java security module is used to develop a file encryption mechanism.

UrSpace is dynamicly updated software with a steady flow of frequent updates. In order to ensure users have access to the latest version, UrSpace comes equipped with on-line software renew option. This function downloads and installs the latest UrSpace updates from the DARB website.

Figure 2: UrSpace Tool Layout

The Scheduler depicted in Figure 3 lets users set their own update schedule, in order to ensure updates do not interfere with personal workload.

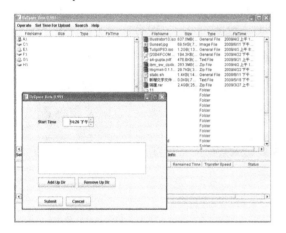

Figure 3: UrSpace Scheduler

3.2 UrSpace Components

In addition to providing some common data management functions, the UrSpace tool also contains various user-friendly features. These designs are made up of several different data manipulation components that are able to help users manage their digital archives more easily. As Figure 4 shows, the UrSpace tool has the following components:

• **Data manipulation** – The UrSpace tool supports several basic data manipulation functions, including adding common folders, deleting recursive files, and a data viewer function. Users are able to rename their files or directories with multilingual words. UrSpace can also display basic file information such as file size and the number of files in a folder.

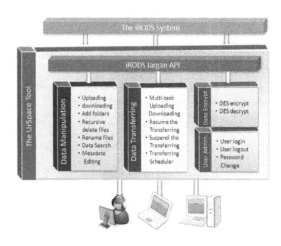

Figure 4: UrSpace Components

• **Data transferring** –The UrSpace tool supports multiple simultaneous data transfers. Users are able to execute several different tasks to upload and download data simultaneously. Moreover, the DARB team designed a mechanism to pause and resume data transfers. This mechanism permits users to suspend their data transfers temporarily.

• **Data encryption** – UrSpace supports the Data Encryption Standard (DES) file encryption. Users can encrypt their digital archives and upload them to the iRODS system. Currently, users are able to download files and decrypt them to a local disk with the UrSpace tool.

• **Data search** – Since the UrSpace tool has a built-in search assistant, users can use file names to search digital archives stored in the iRODS system. The search assistant gives users exact search results including file names, file routes, and file size.

• **Metadata editing** – The iRODS system allows users to register digital archive metadata in an iCAT (iRODS Catalog). Thus, UrSpace provides users with a metadata editing assistant. This assistant lets users browse, add and modify metadata on-line.

4. The Sync Package

The Sync Package provides users with another option for managing their digital archives. It is true that the UrSpace tool includes many data manipulation functions that help users preserve their data more conveniently. However, the Sync Package utility is focused more on developing the automatic data synchronization and efficient data preservation methods. According to user surveys, many users have several very specific needs. For example, some users need to mass upload large digital archives all at one time, while others would like their archives to upload and backup data automatically. Furthermore, some users need detailed data transfer logs.

In order to meet these needs, the Sync Package was developed. In order to help with mass uploading large digital archives, the package uses parallel I/O techniques to improve data transfer speeds. Moreover, users can operate the Sync Package in coordination with the OS scheduler to synchronize data automatically. The package also makes use of an e-mail dispatcher program that is able to send data synchronization records to users via e-mail. Lastly, the sync package includes file encryption and UTF8 encoding conversion. As a result, the Sync Package gives users another way to manage digital archives more efficiently.

4.1 Sync Package Workflows

Figure 5 below demonstrates how the Sync Package implements the helpful features mentioned above. Overall, the process is fairly straightforward. After first setting the iRODS user environment, users should open the main batch file and enter in the data route for the local and remote sites, and then their e-mail address. Now, users may execute the main batch file, and the digital archives will either be uploaded to the iRODS system or downloaded to a local disk space. Users may also integrate this package into an OS scheduling tool so that data backup is handled automatically.

After executing the batch file, the International Language Transform Service will convert the digital archive file names into UTF8 encoding. Depending on the user's needs, the package will either encrypt or decrypt archives, and then upload or download the assigned task. A data record generator records this process as a log file, which is then sent to the user's mailbox.

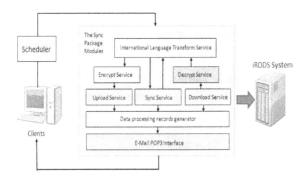

Figure 5 Workflows of the Sync Package

4.2 International Language Support

In order to assist multilingual users, the Sync Package comes equipped with an international language encoding converter. While Taiwan uses traditional Chinese characters, users sometimes label files with Japanese or simplified Chinese characters. In general, multilingual applications convert language text that originated from different sources into UTF8 encoding. However, the Sync Package operates using a command-line, which does not support UTF8 encoding on the Windows operating system. Furthermore, iRODS i-Commands do not provide UTF8

encoding conversion. Thus, an international language encoding converter is needed.

Because iRODS i-Commands are at the core of the Sync Package, the international language encoding converter was embedded within the iRODS i-Command code. The converter contains several different encoding mapping tables, including "Big5", "GBK" and "Shift-JIS". Also, the Big5 table was extended to support Japanese and simplified Chinese characters, so that users can manipulate different language on the traditional Chinese Windows operating system. As Figure 6 shows, when users upload data to the iRODS system, the converter first detects the OS language setting automatically, and selects a suitable encoding mode. It then converts the files into UTF8, and records the value of the file name into the database management system. In the case where users download data to their local sites, the converter inverts the value of the file names with UTF8 encoding from the database to the encoding format of their local OS language setting.

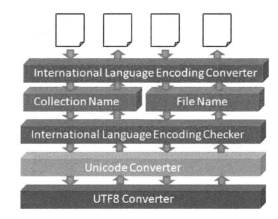

Figure 6 The Workflows of the UTF8 Converter

4.3 Parallel File Encryption

In regards to encryption, the iRODS system uses a GSI security mechanism and constructs a secure data-transferring tunnel. However, the iRODS system does not have a file encryption mechanism, and thus important information from digital archives is vulnerable to theft. In order to protect user data, file encryption was incorporated into the Sync Package. In the beginning, we used a simple symmetric encryption method, called the Data Encryption Standard (DES).

The Sync Package's DES model is the same as the one used within the UrSpace tool, and the DES algorithm is suitable for working in parallel. We implement the DES algorithm in Electronic Codebook (ECB) mode and use the OpenMP API to upgrade the encryption's performance on multi-core CPUs.

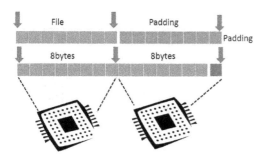

Figure 7 Parallel DES Encryption

As Figure 7 shows, initially, a file is composed of several 8 bytes blocks, and each block is encrypted in parallel. Then, we follow RFC 1423 padding method to affix padding to the encrypted file. Users simply need to fill in their file-encryption password in the main batch file, and then the package encrypts or decrypts their data.

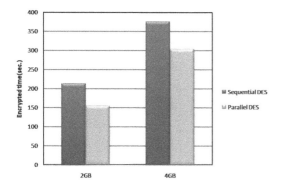

Figure 8 Performance of the Parallel DES encryption

Figure 8 demonstrates that, compared with sequen–tial DES, parallel DES performs on average up to 30% faster on an Intel Duo-Core 3.0GHz CPU.

5. The Monitoring System

The SIMS monitoring system is critical for detecting system problems within iRODS instantly, in order to ensure data loss from disasters is minimal. Developed by the DARB team, SIMS is designed to monitor iRODS as well as the database management system and server operations. After surveying several options, the DARB team settled on Nagios [6] for monitoring distributed environments, largely because it offers several kinds of distributed data management mechanisms. Unfortunately, Nagios does not inherently support the iRODS system, and only provides notification via e-mail. Consequently, the team extended the use of the Nagios monitoring service to monitor the iRODS system. Here, it is important to note that the SIMS monitoring system works independently of the iRODS

system. SIMS records the activities of the server, database, and storage system and then notifies system administrators when an error occurs in the following ways.

5.1 The SIMS Parser

Each iRODS system records its activities in a log file, which keeps track of system processes and error messages. These messages help system administrators troubleshoot and trace problems when errors occur. However, these messages are not always necessary, and thus a parser tool is used to parse messages and identify important communications. For archival purposes, a MySQL database was selected to store records. Overall, the parser helps system administrators receive important messages from a large number of system activities.

5.2 SIMS Notification System

In addition to observing system activities, the monitoring system is supposed to notify system administrators as soon as possible when a system gets into trouble. As mentioned previously, SIMS generally notifies system administrators via e-mail or instant message when receiving an error message. However, for different urgent levels of error messages, the notification mechanisms should not be the same. SIMS utilizes a heartbeat mode to detect if the iRODS system is up and running. In the event that the system is down, SIMS dispatches an urgent message to the system administrators' cell phone. In addition to serious error messages, system administrators are still able to receive error messages from e-mail or instant message.

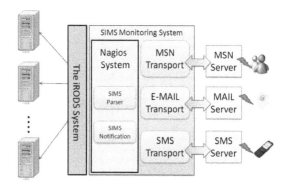

Figure 9 SIMS Notification System

6. Conclusions

Our everyday lives are surrounded by digital data – nearly everything we watch, hear, or read is digital. As the sheer volume of this data continues to grow, users will increasingly encounter problems with storage capacity, data authentication, data integrity, and metadata management. The iRODS system contains several optimized data management mechanisms that address these issues and help users manage digital archives flexibly. While iRODS has its disadvantages, namely the lack of support for UTF8 encoding and file encryption in i-Commands and the absence of a good Jargon API-based multi-function user interface for Chinese, these problems are ameliorated by the inclusion of the UrSpace tool and Sync Package developed by the DARB team. Furthermore, the DARB team will continue to develop these tools, with an emphasis on data management, stability and security.

7. References

[1] Berman, F. "Got data? A guide to data preservation in the information age", Communications of ACM, Vol. 5112 pp.50-6, 2008.

[2] Gantz, J., Chute, C., Mafrediz, Al., Minton, S., Reinsel, D., Schlichting, W., Toncheva, A., "The Diverse and Exploding Digital Universe: An Updated Forecast of Worldwide Information Growth through 2011", white paper, International Data Cooperation, Framingham, MA,2008.

[3] TELDAP Website: http://www.teldap.tw/en/

[4] The iRODS Website: http://www.irods.org

[5] DARB Website: http://rempte-backup.teldap.tw

[6] Nagios Website: http://www.nagios.org

[7] Anjay Ghemawat, Howard Gobioff, and Shun-Tak Leung , "The google file system", 19th ACM Symposium on Operating Systems Principles, 2003.

[8] The Hadoop website: http:// hadoop.apache.org/

[9] Davis WebDAV:https://projects.arcs.org.au/trac/davis/wiki

A GridFTP Interface for iRODS

Shunde Zhang (shunde.zhang@arcs.org.au)
The Australian Research Collaboration Service (ARCS)

Abstract

This paper describes the design and implementation of a GridFTP interface for iRODS, the Integrated Rule-Oriented Data System. Users of the previous Data Intensive Cyber Environments Center (DICE Center) Storage Resource Broker (SRB) may know that there is a GridFTP interface for SRB, written in C as a DSI plugin for the Globus GridFTP server. However, there is no such plugin on Globus GridFTP for iRODS yet. The implementation of this GridFTP interface for iRODS is to provide an OS-independent and standalone solution that doesn't rely on Globus but is compatible with existing Globus clients.

1. Introduction

GridFTP is the de facto standard protocol for data transfer in the grid world. It is based on the traditional FTP protocol with enhanced features for better performance and reliable transfer. Our implementation is a standalone Java-based GridFTP server with Jargon to connect to iRODS. It is self-contained and doesn't require the installation of Globus, which makes it easier to install and run.

2. Features

The current version of this interface mainly follows the specification of GridFTP version 1, and 51 GridFTP commands have been implemented. The main features are listed below.

2.1. Parallel Transfer

In GridFTP version 1, data always flows from the source to the destination. When uploading a file (STOR), it has to be in passive mode (PASV followed by STOR), where the server listens on a port waiting for the client to open multiple connections to it; then the client starts sending data. While doing a download (RETR), it has to be in active mode (PORT, OPTS parallelism, then RETR). In this mode, the client listens on a port and the server opens a number of connections to the client, where the number is specified in the OPTS parallelism command. Then data flows from the server to the client.

The scenario we face is data going from a GridFTP client to a GridFTP server, and then to an iRODS server, or vise versa. We assume that the GridFTP server and the iRODS server are on the same VM/machine, or in the same local network with a fast network connection, while the GridFTP client and the GridFTP server are in different cities with a WAN connection, which is much slower than the GridFTP server to iRODS server connection. Therefore,

the bottleneck is the lag between the GridFTP client and the GridFTP server. In this implementation, we use one connection between the GridFTP server and the iRODS server, and allow multiple connections between the GridFTP client and the GridFTP server. The iRODS protocol does support parallel transfers, but Jargon currently lacks support for that. However, our experiments show that the single connection doesn't affect the whole transfer, based on our assumptions.

2.2. File Operations

Most basic file operations are implemented, including: creating a new folder (MKD), deleting a folder (RMD), file listing (LIST), listing only names (NLST), listing for machine process (MLST and MLSD), renaming a file (RNFR and RNTO), deleting a file (DELE), changing working directory (CWD), printing current directory (PWD), etc.

2.3. Other Transfer Features

Data channel authentication is supported to protect file contents during the transfer. In particular, DCAU A (self authentication) is used by default. It can be turned off by sending a "DCAU N" command. Disabling DCAU can produce better performance.

Performance markers are sent back from the server in extended block mode to monitor the performance. They are also useful for keeping the control channel socket alive as they are sent every 5 seconds, so that the control channel socket will never timeout, even during large file transfers.

2.4. Work in Progress

UDT support is currently under development. UDT has been added to the latest GridFTP 5.0, and has proved to be faster than TCP transfer.

3. Experiments

A simple test of transferring twenty-one 320 Mb files (6.7G in total) from Hobart to Melbourne (using a 310 Mbps connection) shows it performing well.

Test	Time
Globus GridFTP 5 on disk (UDT, 2 FTP connections, 2 threads each)	10.5 mins
Globus GridFTP 5 on disk (TCP, 2 FTP connections, 2 threads each)	15 mins
Griffin to iRODS (TCP, 2 FTP connections, 2 threads each)	14 mins
iput	13 mins

3. iRODS Integration

Enhancing iRODS Integration: Jargon and an Evolving iRODS Service Model

Mike Conway

Data Intensive Cyber Environments Center (DICE Center), University of North Carolina at Chapel Hill

Abstract

Jargon is a pure-Java API that encapsulates an XML protocol defined by the iRODS Data Grid. Jargon allows integration with iRODS [1], and is evolving to provide new integration possibilities. This paper describes planned enhancements to the Jargon API developed by Lucas Gilbert.

Index Keyword Terms—Jargon, Java

1. Introduction

iRODS is described by its creators as a type of "adaptive middleware that provides a flexible, extensible, and customizable data management architecture [2]." The iRODS system facilitates the creation of a distributed data grid across heterogeneous storage platforms. iRODS manages communication, metadata, security, auditing, federation, and other vital aspects of a distributed data grid with a unique policy-based approach. The iRODS system expresses data management policies as rules, which are high-level work-flows. These rules are composed of micro-services, which are small modules that perform data grid operations of various types [3].

Jargon, originally developed by Lucas Gilbert, is a pure Java API that allows thin-client connectivity to the iRODS Data Grid. Jargon handles low-level communication with iRODS using a native XML protocol. This protocol describes the sending of commands and data from a network client, as well as the receiving of status and data from the iRODS system [4]. Currently, Jargon is used to integrate a diverse set of custom applications and frameworks with iRODS.

As the number of grid-enabled applications grows, and as distributed systems evolve, so should the Jargon API. Web services using SOAP and REST are now common [5]. Messaging middleware, workflow tools, custom Java applications written on top of the Jargon API, and custom applications written using dynamic scripting languages are anticipated patterns of Jargon usage. By adhering to open standards and development practices, Jargon will become a useful tool, extending iRODS functionality to a wide array of audiences.

2. Recent Jargon Developments

Jargon is receiving new attention as community demand has grown. Jargon is actively used, therefore, efforts to update Jargon are proceeding carefully. Recent efforts include updating the code base to current standards, introducing unit testing, a large number of bug fixes, and refactoring activities.

3. Assessing Jargon

The most recent Jargon development has been done from the perspective of a developer who had an intermediate knowledge of iRODS, and no prior experience with the Jargon Java API. The experience provided valuable insights that have influenced Jargon development plans. These insights, and the resulting design choices, are the subject of this paper.

First, it must be said that the current Jargon does a very good job of navigating the iRODS XML Protocol. There are a myriad number of details that must be handled, and many of the difficult problems with low-level iRODS communication were solved by Lucas Gilbert in the initial versions of Jargon. The utility of the existing Jargon code is an asset that will enable the future evolution.

A primary issue is that Jargon is difficult to use without in-depth prior knowledge. Much of this is due to the complexity of the problems that iRODS addresses. Even so, Jargon exposes too many of the low-level details of iRODS in the public API.

Over time, Jargon has lost track of current best practices. Examples include the 'hand-rolled' nature of logging in Jargon, the lack of unit testing and measured code coverage, and the lack of a build and dependency management system such as Maven [7]. Many Jargon functions are now better supported in mature open-source libraries. One example is the Jargon support for HTTP file systems, which is significantly less capable than the Apache HTTP Client library [8].

Jargon has evolved to a point where refactoring is necessary. Small steps have already been taken, and will increase as releases proceed. This refactoring and enhancement will produce a set of libraries and capabilities to achieve Jargon's goals.

4. Jargon goals

4.1. Higher Level API

A primary goal in designing a follow-on version of Jargon will be to more effectively hide low-level details from API users. Only a few packages for domain objects and services should be presented to users as the public API, and there should only be one route to accomplish a task. This means that any reference to the iRODS XML protocol, or any semantics about connections or thread-safety should be hidden. The ideal would be a service level API, and interaction using familiar POJO's to represent domain data and actions. The strategy should be to leverage the existing Jargon code as much as possible, as there is a significant accumulation of real-world experience reflected in the code.

4.2. Enabling Familiar Development Practices

One important 'target audience' for Jargon will be a developer in another domain who is not intimately familiar with iRODS. This will likely be a developer who is used to developing web-facing or web service applications using existing best practices.

These practices should be reflected in the code, including:

- An "inversion of control" [8] pattern and development using the de-facto standard Spring container [9].
- The use of "POJO's" (Plain-Old-Java-Objects) [10].
- Facilities to enable test-driven development.
- Use of common build management practices, familiar libraries for logging, and other common practices.

4.3. Providing an Out-of-the-box Administrative and Archivist' Interface

iRODS has a large suite of tools, and a well-defined low-level interface. Like the Unix shell, icommands provide a knowledgeable user with a quick path to desired functionality [11], but can present some difficulty to occasional users. As the user base grows in size and diversity, it cannot be assumed that all users of iRODS will want to work with their data grid in this manner. It has become a common expectation that there will be web-based tools to interact with middleware platforms, including iRODS. A new, out-of-the-box administrative and archivist's interface is being developed on top of Jargon. The working name of this facility is "Jargon-Lingo". At the time of this writing, a full-stack working prototype has been developed.

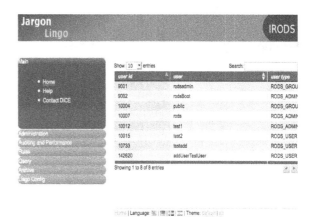

Figure 1 - Jargon web administrative interface

4.4 Enabling iRODS Integration

iRODS itself has many facilities for integration, including a driver architecture that allows many different storage types, and the ability to integrate databases and data streams into the grid. Jargon will provide an even richer integration environment at multiple levels:

- Java API level integration utilizing Jargon core libraries directly in custom applications. An example is the PoDRI project at UNC, which is integrating iRODS with DuraSpace using the Akubra API [12].
- Integration with dynamic scripting languages leveraging JVM dynamic language capabilities [13].
- Service integration with REST and SOAP interfaces on top of Jargon. An example is the integration of iRODS functionality with the Islandora project [14], where PHP scripts could act on the iRODS Data Grid using a service API.
- Integration of iRODS services in emerging cloud computing frameworks, such as jclouds [15].

In addition to the proposed Administrative and Archivist's interface, there will be a large number of custom interfaces for specific purposes. An example of this is an ongoing project to integrate the Islandora [11] Drupal module with iRODS, providing a simple, clean interface for many audiences.

5. Proposed Jargon Architecture

The following diagram illustrates the current Jargon design model, and reflects the above stated observations and goals. The remainder of this paper will discuss the properties of the proposed technology stack.

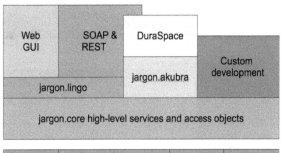

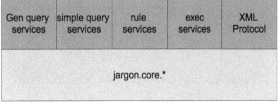

Figure 2 -Proposed Jargon Architecture

Jargon will evolve into a layered architecture, providing a clean separation of concerns, easier extension, and more effective testing through small, mockable units. Jargon will also move forward with the goal of effective test coverage at each level, providing a dependable toolkit as iRODS versions progress.

5.1. jargon.core.*

At the base of the API are the jargon.core libraries. Jargon, as it currently exists, will be transformed over time to become part of the low-level facilities in jargon.core, and this API will be made invisible to public users. Jargon refactoring activities have already begun, and will continue with the jargon.core model in mind.

Networking and low-level protocol handling will be encapsulated at this level, and this should enable easier optimization and tuning while shielding users from API changes. The development of a test suite dedicated to exercising the full iRODS XML at this level protocol will be of great assistance in validating Jargon-based applications as successive iRODS versions are developed.

The primary entry point into the jargon.core functionality will be an iRODSProtocol object that encapsulates the raw network connection to iRODS, as well as the passing to and receiving of messages from the iRODS agent. Also, at this API level, the Jargon prototype includes new facilities for creating and keeping connections such that pooling and caching strategies can be plugged in. No code above the base jargon.core library will access the network connections to iRODS, and will only deal with XML messages.

5.2. jargon.core Mid-level Services

Above the infrastructure that handles connections to iRODS will be a set of mid level services. This intermediate layer will represent the major types of interactions that a client may have with iRODS. The jargon.core mid-level services are not a part of the public API, but do define common capabilities that can be combined by higher level services. Service will include:

- General Query Service – Provides a JDBC like interface to submit SQL-like queries and receive results resembling a JDBC ResultSet. The requests are for pre-defined columns using pre-defined relationships, and mirror the capabilities of the "iquest" icommand.
- Simple Query Service – Executes specific SQL statements permitted by iRODS and receives results resembling a JDBC ResultSet. This is somewhat like General Query, however, it can be used for more complex queries. Simple Query requires permitted SQL to be defined on the iRODS Server. Simple Query services can be used to optimize certain Jargon operations as the need arises.
- Rule Service – Executes rules on iRODS and return results. A philosophy in Jargon development is to use native iRODS functionality, as close to the data as possible, to deliver services to clients.
- Execution Service – Executes arbitrary scripts on an iRODS server from a known location.
- XML Protocol Actions – Executes actions, such as updates, and file operations using specific methods in the iRODS XML Protocol.

5.3. Connection Handling

The current Jargon code base attempts to share a connection between multiple threads, but since those threads access one common socket, the communications occur in a serialized fashion. One side effect of the current connection scheme in Jargon is that the "Command" class is forced to contain all the Jargon functionality in one place, with various levels of synchronization. Testing with the current arrangement, using VisualVM [16], reveals the following pattern for multiple threads sharing a connection in the current Jargon:

Figure 3 – Multiple threads sharing a connection

As you can see, even though multiple threads are accessing the connection, the actual communication with iRODS is single-threaded. The complications this multi-threaded connection access causes are clear, and the benefits of such sharing is doubtful. The relative efficiency of a connection per thread versus attempting to share a connection between multiple threads is an important area for study and testing, especially with connection pooling capability added to Jargon.

5.4. Access Objects

Jargon development should provide a familiar experience to Java mid-tier developers. One way to achieve that goal will be to utilize familiar design patterns. An added benefit will be that such design patterns have been battle-tested in many application deployments.

A primary design pattern for data enabled applications is the DAO Pattern [17]. As Sun describes this pattern in the J2EE Patterns Catalog:

"Use a Data Access Object (DAO) to abstract and encapsulate all access to the data source. The DAO manages the connection with the data source to obtain and store data."

The Jargon prototype uses an adaptation of the DAO pattern that is defined as a Jargon "Access Object". The Access Object framework will:

- Allow creation of Access Objects from a factory.
- Manage connection sharing such that multiple Access Objects in one thread may automatically utilize the same connection.
- Utilize jargon.core mid-tier services to accomplish tasks, and shield API users from details of each Access Object method.
- Use POJO domain objects for parameters and return values.

The concept of an "Access Object" in Jargon is inspired by a very common pattern of development using DAO objects and POJO domain objects with Hibernate [18]. The handling of session in Hibernate DAO's via a ThreadLocal Session object provides an attractive model for a cleaner codebase, treating an iRODS connection in a manner similar to a familiar JDBC connection to a database.

Jargon Access Objects are the lowest level of publicly usable API. Access Objects can be combined into higher level services, both within the Jargon API, and externally, by developers wishing to create new functionality. The following code snippet shows a User access object that utilizes a mid-level General Query service, and returns a User domain object.

```
public User findById(final String userId) throws
JargonException,DataNotFoundException {

    iRODSGenQueryExecutorImpl iRODSGenQueryExecutorImpl
        = new iRODSGenQueryExecutorImpl(

    this.getiRODSProtocol());
    StringBuilder userQuery = new StringBuilder();

    userQuery.append(buildUserSelects());
    userQuery.append(" where ");

    userQuery.append(RodsGenQueryEnum.COL_USER_ID
        .getName);
    userQuery.append(" = '");
    userQuery.append(userId);
    userQuery.append("'");


            . . .

    iRODSQuery iRODSQuery
    iRODSQuery.instance(userQueryString, 500, 0);
    iRODSQueryResultSet resultSet;
    resultSet = iRODSGenQueryExecutorImpl
        .executeiRODSQuery(iRODSQuery,0);


            . . .

    List<String> row = resultSet.getResults().get(0);
    User user = buildUserFromResultSet(row);

    return user;

}
```

This example Access Object illustrates a clean, higher-level object upon which services may be built. It is important to note that connection handling in this example is transparent, that no low-level protocol operations are visible at this layer, and that the operations of this method are easily tested with mock objects. This example also illustrates how Access Objects like this User Access Object make use of mid-level services, in this case a General Query Service. That General Query Service, in turn, relies on low-level jargon.core packages to turn the query into an XML protocol request, communicate the request to iRODS, and turn the XML protocol response from iRODS into a manageable object that resembles a familiar JDBC ResultSet for processing by the Access Object. Importantly, the caller of this Access Object does not see the underlying ResultSet, rather, the findUserById() method returns a POJO User object.

5.5 A Jargon Service Model

High-level Jargon services can be easily exposed as SOAP and REST using commodity open-source middleware such as Spring Web Services [19], Apache Axis [20], and Metro [21]. As lower level services are developed and tested, consideration will need to be given to the design of a REST/SOAP service model. This service model will allow iRODS to interact with a large number of external systems, and will be developed in the jargon.lingo libraries. The development of a service model is beyond the scope of this document, however, the Spring framework that is powering the web administrative GUI prototype would be a potential provider of REST-ful services, and would likely will not present a high technical hurdle. The Fedora Repository service model provides an excellent model for similar iRODS services [22].

Prototypes under development validate the basic approach outlined in this document, and it can be said with a level of confidence that a Jargon-based service layer providing both SOAP and REST-ful access to iRODS is quite feasible. Beyond the remaining technical hurdles, much consideration needs to be given to the use-cases, security model, and implications of such a facility.

6. Conclusion

This paper outlines some of the high-level design goals, and a proposed architecture for future Jargon development. At the writing of this paper, a working prototype does exist, and is being used for validation and experimentation. While still a work in progress, the prototype does provide valuable guidance for near-term Jargon refactoring. Jargon development will be guided by careful testing, community input, and current best practices.

Jargon, and the integration possibilities that it will enable, has the goal of making the iRODS Data Grid as familiar to developers as a database or messaging middleware platform, and a dependable tool to help manage the expanding need for secure sharing and preservation of data.

7. References

1. Jargon, A Java client API for the DataGrid, https://www.iRODS.org/index.php/Jargon
2. iRODS: integrated Rule Oriented Data System White Paper Data Intensive Cyber Environments Group University of North Carolina at Chapel Hill University of California at San Diego September 2008 Rajasekar, A., M. Wan, R. Moore, W. Schroeder
3. iRODS: integrated Rule-based Data System Rajasekar, A., M. Wan, R. Moore, W. Schroeder
4. *Packing/Unpacking Scheme Used in iRODS* Mike Wan, DICE
5. Restful web services vs." big"'web services: making the right architectural decision http://www2008.org/papers/pdf/p805-pautassoA.pdf [PDF]
C Pautasso, O Zimmermann, F Leymann - 2008 – portal.acm.org
6. Apache Maven, http://maven.apache.org/
7. Apache HTTP Client , http://hc.apache.org/httpclient-3.x
8. Inversion of control containers and the dependency injection pattern, http://www.itu.dk/courses/VOP/E2006/8_injection.pdf [PDF], M Fowler - Actualizado el – itu.dk
9. Spring Framework, http://www.springsource.org/
10. Christopher Richardson, "What is POJO Programming?", Java Developer's Journal, http://java.sys-con.com/node/180374
11. iRODS icommands, https://www.iRODS.org/index.php/icommands
12. Akubra Project, http://www.fedora-commons.org/confluence/display/AKUBRA/Akubra+Project
13. New JDK 7 Feature: Support for Dynamically Typed Languages in the Java Virtual Machine, http://java.sun.com/developer/technicalArticles/DynTypeLang/
14. Islandora Project, http://islandora.ca/
15. jclouds framework, http://code.google.com/p/jclouds/
16. VisualVM, http://java.sun.com/javase/6/docs/technotes/guides/visualvm/
17. DAO Pattern, http://java.sun.com/blueprints/corej2eepatterns/Patterns/DataAccessObject.html
18. Generic Data Access Objects, https://www.hibernate.org/328.html
19. Spring Web Services, http://static.springsource.org/spring-ws/sites/1.5/
20. Apache Axis, http://ws.apache.org/axis/
21. Metro Web Services Framework, https://metro.dev.java.net/
22. Fedora Service Framework, http://fedora-commons.org/confluence/display/FCR30/Service+Framework

Appendices

Appendix 1: Agenda of the iRODS User Group Meeting 2010

iRODS User Meeting Agenda

March 24 – 26, 2010 at Renaissance Computing Institute, UNC, Chapel Hill NC

Wednesday, March 24

Session I (9:00- 10:30)
- **Introduction to iRODS** (30 min) Moore
- **iRODS Version 2.3** (30 min) Schroeder
- **Introduction to Micro-services** (30 min) Moore

Break (30 min)

Session II (11:00-12:30)
- **Intro to Policies** (30 min) Moore
- **Policy session,** how to build a set of policies for your collection (1 hour) Rajasekar

Lunch **(**12:30 – 1:30)

Session III (1:30- 3:00)
- **Micro-service session,** how to write a micro-service (1 hour) Wan
- **Advanced iCommands** (30 min) Wan

Break (30 min)

Session IV (3:30-5:00)
- **iCAT interactions** (1 hour) Schroeder / Rajasekar
- **Questions** (30 min)

Thursday, March 25

Session V (9:00-10:30)
- **User Application Sessions, How Communities Have Applied iRODS**
  - *High Availability iRODS System (HAIRS)* Yutaka Kawai (KEK, Japan), Adil Hasan (University of Liverpool) (teleconference)
  - *iRODS at CC-IN2P3* Jean-Yves Nief, Pascal Calvat, Yonny Cardenas, Pierre-Yves Jallud, Thomas Kachelhoffer (CC-IN2P3, Lyon, France)
  - *Using iRODS to Preserve and Publish a Dataverse Archive*, Mason Chua (Odum Institute, UNC), Antoine de Torcy (DICE, UNC), Jewel H. Ward (SILS, UNC), Jonathan Crabtree (Odum Institute, UNC)
  - *Distributed Data Sharing with PetaShare for Collaborative Research*, PetaShare Team @LSU (poster)
  - *University of North Carolina Information Technology Services*, William Schultz (UNC) (poster)

Break (30 Min)

Thursday (cont.)
Session VI (11:00-12:30)

- o *The ARCS Data Fabric*, Shunde Zhang, Florian Goessmann, Pauline Mak (ARCS) (poster)
- o *A Service-Oriented Interface to the iRODS Data Grid*, Nicola Venuti, Francesco Locunto (NICE), Michael Conway, Leesa Brieger (DICE RENCI UNC)
- o *iExplore for iRODS Distributed Data Management*, Bing Zhu (DICE UCSD)
- o *A GridFTP Interface for iRODS*, Shunde Zhang (ARCS)

Lunch (12:30-1:30)

Session VII (1:30-3:00)
- • **Clients for iRODS**
  - o *The Development of Digital Archives Management Tools for iRODS,* Tsung-Tai Yeh, Hsin-Wen Wei, Shin-Hao Liu (Academia Sinica, Taiwan), Pei-Chi Huang (Tsing Hua University, Taiwan), Tsan-sheng Hsu (Academia Sinica, Taiwan), Yen-Chiu Chen (Tsing Hua University, Taiwan)
  - o *Building a Trusted Distributed Archival Preservation Service with iRODS*, Jewel H. Ward, Terrell G. Russell, and Alexandra Chassanoff (SILS, UNC) (poster)
  - o *Conceptualizing Policy-Driven Repository Interoperability (PoDRI) Using iRODS and Fedora*, David Pcolar (CDR, UNC), Daniel W. Davis (Cornell, DuraSpace), Bing Zhu (DICE UCSD), Alexandra Chassanoff (SILS, UNC), Chien-Yi Hou, Richard Marciano (SALT, UNC)
  - o *Community-Driven Development of Preservation Services*, Richard Marciano (SALT, UNC), Chien-Yi Hou (SALT, UNC), Jennifer Ricker (NC State Library), Glen McAninch (KY Dept. Lib. & Archives), David Pcolar (CDR, UNC) et al.

Break (30 min)
Session VIII (3:30-5:00)
- o *Enhancing iRODS Integration: Jargon and an Evolving iRODS Service Model* Mike Conway (DICE, UNC)
- o Questions on user porting of clients

Friday, March 26

Session IX (9:00-10:30)
- • **Prioritization of tasks** (1 1/2 hour) Moore

Break (30 min)

Session X (11:00-12:30)
- • **Question and Answers** (1 1/2 hours) Moore

Lunch (12:30 – 1:30)

Session XI (1:30 – 3:00)
- • **Integration Session,** how to integrate your favorite workflow/client with iRODS (60 min) Conway
- • **Data Intensive Cyberinfrastructure Foundation session,** coordinating development across interested communities. (30 minutes) Tooby

Appendix 2: iRODS Requested Features

<table-center> **iRODS Requested Features** Key: B = Bug A = Completed Number = No. of user group requests (0 indicates requests by users not present, etc.) </table-center>	
B	Add a Doxygen indexed version of iRODS source on the wiki for micro-services and helper functions.
B	Add object type to audit trail
B	Allow GSI authentication to non-ICAT-Enabled-Server without irodsUserName being set.
	Automate Dicom metadata extraction from binary files. Find misextractdicom
B	Fix UDP on Solaris.
B	Implement FITS header parsing and metadata loading. Find msiextractfits
B	Issues with symbolic links on FUSE mounted directory - copy symbolic links when directory structure is ignored
B	Post link to VBrowser, links to Taverna and EGEE grid
B	Post on Wiki a list of the planned developments for Jargon.
B	Publish the complete iRODS network protocol.
18	Admin interface to list all current connections and the associated irods users. (keep with record of IP addresses)
16	Set access controls on rules and micro-services. Currently on users, collections, resources, metadata.
15	Editorial review of documentation
15	Document all APIs
15	icommand for checking ports (health check). Jargon admin will do this
15	icommands with tab completion
15	Installation - check for firewall interaction (notification of presence, like a ping on each port).
15	Links to Petashare, Urspace, Jux, 43 clients
15	Script for checking/updating IP address (5 locations).
15	Support transfer of multiple files using multiple I/O streams. Virtual ibun
12	Add regular expressions to i-commands (wild cards).
12	Use external identity management and external authentication
11	Management of rules within iCAT to enable versioning. Distribution of rules to core.irb file at each server.
11	Request for Shibboleth based authentication for new users (UNC) credential mapping / assign privilege according to Shibboleth role - TUCASI
10	A more general mechanism to access external databases. Admin will define location and specify SQL, client will be able to provide arguments. Independent of ICAT. Need a way for the information provided, or saved, to be integrated into the iRODS framework.
10	Add -P to irsync
10	Support for accented letters (metadata and filenames) - Taiwan
10	Support for dynamic IP address.
9	Export audit trails from iCAT and truncate
9	Have second notification list about upgrades that address vulnerabilities. Set up an iRODS admin mailing list.
9	irsync across physical resources to repair corruption - similar to irepl
9	Support for Java-based micro-services.
8	Multi-thread connection.
8	Policy consensus development

iRODS Requested Features

Key: B = Bug A = Completed   Number = No. of user group requests
(0 indicates requests by users not present, etc.)

8	SHA-256 checksum, CRC checksum
8	Support checksums in Jargon (before transfer), iput -k
7	Add ability for a project PI to create rodsuser accounts for project members. Create accounts under groupadmin
7	Control number of connections on servers (batch jobs) - connection pool
7	Provide transaction based interaction with external workflow
7	Restrict ability of ASSIGN to change user name, user role, user permissions.
7	Support read-only view on selected columns in database
7	Use defined SQL commands that can be invoked through a micro-service.
7	Virtual ibun that concatenates files for transmission
7	Automatic failover to a secondary iCAT
6	Document the scheduling of rules in parallel, and use of delayed rules
6	Restart rule engine
6	Reload option for irodsctl script to behave like Apache reload
6	Active directory integration with Kerberos, documentation - Chris Jordan
6	Add ways to handle the comment fields for data, resources, users, metadata (icommand and micro-service)
6	Collaborator analysis tool for iRODS community
6	Create script for automating module creation. Provide default template for creating new Micro-service. Documentation
6	iDisk for iRODS - iDrop. The iDisk area is on your computer, and reliably synchs to a remote storage system periodically.
6	Implement queuing/client-backoff within Jargon
6	Manage list of connecting IP addresses to track denial of service
6	Manage queue of requests. Want to control maximum number of executing requests.
6	Metadata analysis tools for federated data grids
6	National dropbox. This is similar to iDisk, and provides a way to back up or share your files through a drag and drop interface.
6	Project analysis tools for domains using iRODS
5	Add AVU metadata to resource groups.
5	Create a Windows only environment, using SqlServer
5	Integration of logging into Jargon
5	Want to disable triggering of rules from a client by selected users
4	Ensure end-to-end audit of data sharing policy for pulling data into a secure environment
4	Federation of independent databases: NC B-prepared / EPA / structured information resource drivers
4	Integration with local metadata (schema), for remote database access
4	Integration with VCL policies - policy engine controlled by metadata, which constructs environment
4	Need drivers for a wide variety of databases for resources
4	Provide mechanism to synchronize rule bases across servers within a data grid.
4	Provide versioning support for rules.
4	Support a session shell in iRODS for iRODS comands, isession. Authenticate once.
4	Support adaptable security policies (change level of access based on situation).

	iRODS Requested Features

iRODS Requested Features

Key: B = Bug A = Completed   Number = No. of user group requests

(0 indicates requests by users not present, etc.)

4	Support local policy enforcement on database access (de-identification)
4	Support Perl-based Micro-services by including Perl interpreter in the Micro-service.
3	Create a Windows only environment, using Postgres and GSI (both now run on Windows)
3	List system generated metadata in iEXP
2	Admin interface to rename a resource.
2	Configure port numbers for data transfer. Support alternate IP address.
2	Driver for other types of databases for use by iCAT (DB2, SQLServer)
2	Native encryption of files, probably through remote execution. Transforms on data.
1	Add core.irb rule to check policy on iget. May want to return alternate version (redacted copy) of file.
1	Are there CIM common information models for accessing databases?
1	Automate creation of an account for new users. Example is GSI based access. Extend to LDAP/Kerberos
1	Create a VM build for use of iRODS in tutorials.
1	Decompress on the fly.
1	iRODS server for memory cache, RAM disk
1	Mechanism to test whether a community's client is compatible with iRODS protocol and version numbers
1	Modify icommands to use the zoneID:internal ID instead of the file name or add GUID
1	Provide a library of script-based micro-services
1	Support compressed files on disk to minimize space. Could be done through a preProcForPut core.irb hook.
1	Support ticket-based access to iRODS.
1	When fail over to an alternate server, verify that the Rule engine will not have a conflict for a queued Micro-service. Related to versioning of rules and micro-services.
0	Create a VDT (Virtual Data Toolkit) version of iRODS.
0	Create digital signing registration to be able to track origin of files. Given signature, find original copy. Related to definition of an AIP
0	Create RDA interface to Sybase.
0	Develop Fortran API.
0	Develop Perl API.
0	Extensions to Jargon for UDP transport.
0	Improve webDAV caching of a working copy of a file correctly
0	Improve webDAV caching of a working copy of a file correctly (external)
0	Manage locks for collaborative editing (either on storage system, in metadata, or portal) - expensive
0	Port iCAT to Sybase.
0	Port SRB APIs on top of iRODS, will avoid having to rewrite many application scripts.
0	Port SRB scommands onto iRODS (remap options)
0	Support logical registration into iRODS. Ability to associate metadata with a name without requiring a file. Add an info file.
0	Support token-based identification such as SecureID. One-time passwords - offload to external authentication management
0	Which types of databases need to be supported?

	iRODS Requested Features
	Key: B = Bug A = Completed Number = No. of user group requests (0 indicates requests by users not present, etc.)
	Completed Tasks
A	Add links to WebDav environment on iRODS wiki, provides drag and drop access to files across windows.
A	Command to force execution on another server. msiremoteexec
A	Consider use of Google Code repository and other shareware sites. Automate. GitHub (Russell)
A	Create a collaboration environment for promoting development of iRODS. (done through DICF)
A	Create a Condor interface / port for iRODS (Stork)
A	For SRB to iRODS metadata migration, handle migration of SRB zones. How can multiple SRB zones be re-federated within iRODS easily? Limited scripts.
A	Hook for preProcForPut for medical applications.
A	icp between data grids (bug fixed)
A	Jargon parallel I/O
A	Mount a flash drive. Treat as a mounted collection.
A	Option to restrict irods admin access to specific hostnames/IP addresses.
A	Provide mechanism to add rule base extensions to a remote rule base.
A	Recursive upload of directories - icommands
A	Save RDA request results for use in a session, want to pass result list to another Micro-service. Put in a file.
A	Support mounting of a Webdav directory into iRODS. (done through DAVIS)
A	Support Python-based Micro-services by including Python interpreter in the Micro-service. Documentation
A	Support sequential transfers as one-hop, similar to parallel. Done for iput.
A	Support Soft Links in iRODS (supported in 2.3)
A	When compile, verify that only changed files are recompiled.

Appendix 3: iRODS Clients

	iRODS Clients Extending Interoperabililty		
	Client	**Developer**	**Language**
1.	Akubra/iRODS	DICE	Jargon
2.	Archive tools-NOAO	Eric – NOAO	
3.	Big Board visualization / FUSE	RENCI	
4.	C API	Mike Wan DICE	C
5.	C I/O library	Wayne Schroeder DICE	C
6.	Davis - WebDAV	ARCS Australia	Jargon
7.	DCAPE	UNC	
8.	Dropbox / iDisk / iDrop	Mike Conway	Jargon
9.	EnginFrame - Jargon	NICE / RENCI	Jargon
10.	Fedora on Fuse	IN2P3 France	FUSE
11.	Fedora/iRODS module	ITS - UNC-CH, DICE	Jargon
12.	File-format-identifier	GA Tech	
13.	FUSE	IN2P3, DICE	FUSE
14.	FUSE optimization	PetaShare LSU	FUSE
15.	GridFTP - Griffin	ARCS Australia	
16.	iExplore	Bing Zhu DICE	C++
17.	Islandora	DICE	Jargon
18.	Jargon	DICE	Jargon
19.	Jsaga	IN2P3 France	Jargon
20.	JUX	IN2P3 France	Jargon
21.	Kepler	DICE	Jargon
22.	OpenDAP	ARCS, Australia	
23.	Parrot	Doug Thain	
24.	Pcommands	PetaShare LSU	
25.	Peta Web browser	PetaShare LSU	
26.	PetaFS (Fuse)	PetaShare team LSU	
27.	Petashell (Parrot)	PetaShare LSU	
28.	PHP - DICE	Bing Zhu, DICE	
29.	Pyrods - Python	Jerome Fusillier	Python
30.	Resource Monitoring	IN2P3	
31.	Saga	KEK	
32.	Shibboleth	King's College, London UK	
33.	Sync-package	Academica Sinica, Taiwan	
34.	Taverna	RENCI	
35.	URSpace	Teldap - Academica Sinica	
36.	VOSpace	IVOA	

iRODS Client Requests		
Admin interface		Jargon
Chronopolis status interface	NCAR	
Earth System Grid publisher	NCAR	
icommands with tab completion		C
iRULE designer	Jerome Fusillier	
Perl load library		
Ruby		
WSDL web service		Jargon
iRODS Micro-services		
Cheshire3	SHAMAN EU	Python
GridFTP	Dresden	
Kepler		
MakeFlow		C

Information on iRODS

iRODS Integrated Rule-Oriented Data System wiki irods.org
Data Intensive Cyber Environments Center at UNC dice.unc.edu
Data Intensive Cyberinfrastructure Foundation diceresearch.org

Books on iRODS

iRODS Primer: Integrated Rule-Oriented Data System

Synthesis Lectures on Information Concepts, Retrieval, and Services

Morgan & Claypool, 2010, 143 pages
doi:10.2200/S00233ED1V01Y200912ICR012
ISBN-10: 1608453332
ISBN-13: 978-1608453337

Abstract

Policy-based data management enables the creation of community-specific collections. Every collection is created for a purpose. The purpose defines the set of properties that will be associated with the collection. The properties are enforced by management policies that control the execution of procedures that are applied whenever data are ingested or accessed. The procedures generate state information that defines the outcome of enforcing the management policy. The state information can be queried to validate assessment criteria and verify that the required collection properties have been conserved. The integrated Rule-Oriented Data System implements the data management framework required to support policy-based data management. Policies are turned into computer actionable Rules. Procedures are composed from a Micro-service-oriented architecture. The result is a highly extensible and tunable system that can enforce management policies, automate administrative tasks, and periodically validate assessment criteria.

Table of Contents: Introduction / Integrated Rule-Oriented Data System / iRODS Architecture / Rule-Oriented Programming / The iRODS Rule System / iRODS Micro-services / Example Rules / Extending iRODS / Appendix A: iRODS Shell Commands / Appendix B: Rulegen Grammar / Appendix C: Exercises / Author Biographies

Proceedings iRODS User Group Meeting 2010
Data Intensive Cyberinfrastructure Foundation
For a PDF of this Proceedings see diceresearch.org

www.ingramcontent.com/pod-product-compliance
Lightning Source LLC
Chambersburg PA
CBHW060458060326
40689CB00020B/4569